Beyond Trauma:
Hope and Healing for Warriors
A Guide for Pastoral Caregivers on Post-traumatic Stress

PRAISE FOR *BEYOND TRAUMA: HOPE AND HEALING FOR WARRIORS*:

Chaplain Dean Bonura brings to the topic of PTSD extensive in-depth knowledge, significant firsthand experience, and secondary experiences as a caregiver. Much has been written about PTSD in recent years; some of the articles and books are very good, and others are mediocre. What Bonura does is present a systematic and quite articulate exposition of PTSD, starting with the milieu and causes, then describes the impact and effects it has on both the individual experiencing PTSD as well as to his or her family and circle of friends and colleagues, and concludes with ample information and an effective model for therapeutic praxis. This book will be a major contribution to the current literature on the topic of PTSD and should be read not only by clergy and caregivers of victims of PTSD but also by military leaders in order for them to have a better and clearer understanding of what many of their troops are experiencing.

— Fr. Eugene Kole, OFM, CONV, DMin
Catholic Chaplain to the Military
Langley Air Force Base

In his book Beyond Trauma: Hope and Healing for Warriors, *Dr. Bonura fills a gap that I believe other manuals have left out. This book is a much-needed, Bible-based manual that will prove invaluable in helping chaplains bring the healing power of Christ to bear in trauma ministry. This well-documented and encompassing work provides clear definitions, pertinent statistics, and suggested methodologies of care.* Beyond Trauma *is a must-own for any chaplain or pastor serious about pastoral care to those who are spiritually wounded by trauma.*

— Rev. Arthur Pace
Chaplain (Colonel), U.S. Army, Retired
Executive Director, Armed Services Ministry,
American Bible Society

If I were to recommend one book to promote both a deeper understanding of the spiritual aspects of PTSD and effective resiliency strategies, Beyond Trauma: Hope and Healing for Warriors *would be it. Chaplain (Colonel) Dean Bonura provides a remarkable range of valuable insights and useful information from a faith-based approach, resulting in a brilliantly written work and a must-read for pastors, chaplains, counselors, and pastoral caregivers. While many trauma survivors believe they "can't get over it," this book will undoubtedly help them to grow out of their pain.*

— Dr. Doug Kinder
Chaplain (Colonel), U.S. Army, Retired
Assemblies of God

In this carefully researched, thought-provoking, and insightful book, ostensibly designed for chaplains, clergymen, and Christian counselors, Chaplain Bonura argues that spiritual maladies require spiritual redress. Frankly, from my perspective, with involvement with multiple organizations in service of the military and veterans, I consider this book is not just for the faith-based community but for all of us. My hope and prayer would be that his message receives the attention it rightly deserves.

— John Gately
Lieutenant Colonel, U.S. Army, Retired
Hampton, Virginia

A masterpiece of hope! Clearly, this book is an invaluable tool for assisting individuals with the aftermath of war. I wish we could have had this information at the beginning of Operation Iraqi Freedom (OIF 1). As Dean reveals, feedback from a number of surveys from those returning from war cite the crucial role that their faith played in supporting and sustaining them. No doubt, the book will serve as a useful guide for those with pastoral responsibilities, but it will be equally useful for anyone dealing with PTSD or associated with it. Tremendous comfort is found in eternal security, which is based on faith in Christ, as the Bible states in Ephesians 2:8–9. No one has dealt with more trauma than Christ, who was sustained by God the Holy Spirit, and He endured it for us. Regardless of one's faith or the lack of faith, the importance of the spiritual dimension in providing trauma support cannot be ignored. Dean offers an exceptional read for helping meet such needs. Read it and see for yourself!

— Bradley W. May
Major General, Retired
United States Army

Dean Bonura, an army chaplain with over three decades of experience and significant warrior interaction, presents a well-researched and practical study of post-traumatic stress disorder (PTSD). He masterfully reminds us of the power of a warrior's faith and the potential for healing drawn from biblical models. This world-class guide for pastoral caregivers will help veterans recover from and succeed beyond the effects of PTSD.

— Mike Carkhuff
Colonel, U.S. Army, Retired
Vietnam Veteran

Dean's compassion for Soldiers who suffer with the hidden wounds of war is evident in this practical, faith-based approach to helping those suffering from post-traumatic stress. While Dr. Bonura has done his research, he makes his *insights usable and useful both in the classroom and in personal interaction. He was personally invited to present an earlier version of this revised and expanded material to midcareer chaplains at the U.S. Army Chaplain Center and School, where it was well received. I highly recommend this book to anyone committed to exploring the role of faith in healing those who have borne the fight and have come back wounded in the soul.*

— Kenneth W. Bush
Chaplain (Colonel), U.S. Army, Retired
Director of Training, Programs, and Research
National Conference on Ministry to the Armed Forces;
Former Director of Training and Leader Development at
the U.S. Army Chaplain Center and School

Drawing from his own research interviewing those with PTSD, as well as from his own experience as an army chaplain who has both helped others and experienced posttraumatic stress himself, Dr. Bonura has written a clear, practical, and biblical resource. He makes a convincing case for the fundamental spiritual dynamics of PTSD, which requires a spiritual response to address effectively. While fellow military chaplains will benefit from this book, civilian pastors dealing with those in their congregations with PTSD will find it particularly helpful in enabling them to identify its signs and provide appropriate pastoral responses. I am delighted to recommend it.

— David A. Currie, MDiv, PhD
Director of the Doctor of Ministry Program;
Associate Professor of Pastoral Theology
Gordon-Conwell Theological Seminary

Society asks much of its warriors who often suffer from the brutal effects of combat. In Beyond Trauma: Hope and Healing for Warriors, *Chaplain Bonura provides a thoroughly researched and experience-based treatment approach for the spiritual effects of trauma. He carefully distinguishes between psychological and spiritual wounds and outlines how these "below-the-waterline" issues can be treated from a Judeo-Christian perspective. Behavioral health specialists are not typically trained to treat issues of the spirit and soul; that is the realm of pastors, chaplains, and counselors trained in pastoral care. This book helps clergy know their lane when treating veterans suffering from the effects of war, allowing for a more effective multidisciplinary approach to healing combat trauma.*

— Andy Meverden
Chaplain (Colonel), U.S. Army, Retired
Colorado National Guard and Director of Chaplaincy,
CB America

Beyond Trauma:
Hope and Healing for Warriors
A Guide for Pastoral Caregivers on Post-traumatic Stress

Dean Bonura
Chaplain (Colonel), U.S. Army (Ret)

Copyright page continued on page 250.

ISBN 978 1-7330962-0-1

Printed and bound in the United States of America

Beyond Trauma: Hope and Healing for Warriors was originally published by WestBow Press, A Division of Thomas Nelson & Zondervan.

Published by the The Warrior's Journey® in partnership with Three Clicks Publishing.
3003 E. Chestnut Expressway Ste 2001
Springfield, MO 65802

thewarriorsjourney.org

To warriors who know the lingering pain of war

and to
the memory of my father,
John J. Bonura

World War II — U.S. Army Veteran — China-Burma-India Theater
February 16, 1925 to May 20, 2015

TABLE OF CONTENTS

FIGURES

PREFACE

In the summer of 2004, I was leaving Iraq after a year of combat in and around the cities of Baghdad, Karbala, and Najaf. Our brigade combat team had suffered twenty-four killed in action (KIA) and more than two hundred wounded in action (WIA). The 1st Armored Division, our higher headquarters, under the leadership of Major General Martin Dempsey, lost 133 Soldiers to combat-related deaths. We were now preparing to return to Germany, which was home to the division at the time. Chaplains in the brigade had the responsibility to prepare our Soldiers for the challenges of returning to their families. So we developed several briefings to prepare them for redeployment and help them with their readjustment and homecoming.

Homecoming, or *reintegration*, as the Army calls it, is a daunting task. In many respects, it's more challenging than combat. Servicemembers return to families that have changed, to spouses who have had to manage households by themselves, to marriages that are in trouble, and to children who have grown up over the last year without their deployed parents. Yes, we all changed. None of us was returning to the way things were. We were returning to the way things had become. And it was our task, as chaplains, to facilitate a new normal for our servicemembers and their families upon our return.

During this time, it occurred to me that I was not very prepared to assist our Soldiers and their families with the aftermath of war. War is traumatic, and I had no clue about the postwar trauma effects that our Soldiers would exhibit upon their return. I remember telling the Soldiers of the Ready First Combat Team, "Should you exhibit any symptoms such as sleeplessness, problems with hypervigilance, anger, grief, or guilt, then see someone in mental health. They can help you." At least I hoped they would.

However, I began to realize that many of the issues our service-members would be dealing with were really more spiritual in nature—deeper and existential symptoms like guilt, grief, and shame, as well as questions about the problem of suffering and the loss of meaning and faith. The military clinical system was not prepared to adequately address these challenges, nor were servicemembers very inclined to seek help from mental health professionals. So two years after my return from combat, I began a doctoral program at Gordon-Conwell Theological Seminary to study the problem of combat-related post-traumatic stress (PTS) and post-traumatic stress disorder (PTSD), but focusing my attention on the spiritual dimension of trauma and its post-traumatic stress symptoms. I discovered that while others had also recognized the presence of spiritual symptoms of trauma, few resources were available to address those symptoms.

This book identifies the spiritual symptoms of trauma and offers spiritual remedies for these symptoms. It's based on my own combat experience as well as my personal experience with post-combat stress. It's written primarily as a guide for pastors, chaplains, pastoral counselors, and church leaders who are interested in helping veterans in their churches or as an outreach to them. But anyone interested in the spiritual aspects of trauma will benefit from reading this book. It is not a comprehensive treatise on post-traumatic stress or PTSD, nor is it a clinical exposition on the treatment of PTS/PTSD.

Happily, since I began my study in 2006, more resources have become available on combat-related PTS. Still, there is a need for more resources that address the spiritual effects of trauma from a Christian and biblical point of view. This book is that kind of resource.

In this book you'll learn about the spiritual dimension of trauma and its effects—what I have characterized as "below-the-waterline" symptoms. The book represents the fruit of research that included an extensive review of literature on trauma and spirituality as well as personal interviews I did with Soldiers from all ranks who served in combat. It also reflects my own combat experience and my thirty-three years of military service.

Pastors, chaplains, and Christian counselors typically possess the skills to make spiritual interventions that will assist servicemembers or veterans with the detrimental symptoms of PTS. Clergy have a legitimate healing role alongside clinicians to make appropriate interventions. The contents of this book will equip them with the knowledge and resources to understand the spiritual dimension of trauma, apply biblical remedies, and lead sufferers in their congregations to healing and growth. Those who suffer from PTS can get beyond many of the negative effects of trauma and achieve a new normal that allows for healthy functioning, which will enable them to become people who are stronger and better equipped to deal with the challenges of living.

I'm convinced the appropriate application of this material, along with a confidence placed in the power of the gospel, will bring healing to wounded souls and lead to an improvement in their quality of life. As pastoral caregivers, we must learn about the veteran's experience and be willing to care for him or her, leading and supporting that veteran in any way we can.

Finally, it is my earnest prayer that God will use this work for his glory and, by the light of the gospel, send its healing and illuminating power into the darkest places of the soul so that all who are oppressed might be set at liberty.

Jesus said, "The Spirit of the Lord is upon me, because he has anointed me to proclaim good news to the poor. He has sent me to proclaim liberty to the captives and recovering of sight to the blind, to set at liberty those who are oppressed, to proclaim the year of the Lord's favor" (Luke 4:18–19). Amen.

Dean Bonura
Chaplain (Colonel), U.S. Army
Joint Base Langley-Eustis, Virginia

ACKNOWLEDGMENTS

This book is an adaptation of a dissertation I completed while I was a doctoral student at Gordon-Conwell Theological Seminary. I want to thank Dr. Ken Swetland, my doctoral mentor, for encouraging me to publish an adaptation of the dissertation.

The completion of this book would not have been possible without the assistance of many other people. I am indebted to my friends and colleagues for assisting me in various ways, whether by granting access to Soldiers, collaborating in training, or advising on the contents of the material. I especially want to thank the following men: Chaplain (Major) James Boyle, retired; Chaplain (Colonel) James White, retired; Chaplain (Major) Lewis Messinger; Chaplain (Lieutenant Colonel) Randy Edwards, retired; Chaplain (Colonel) Kenneth Bush, retired; Chaplain (Colonel) Douglas Kinder, retired; and Chaplain (Colonel) Kenneth Sampson, retired. All of them provided tremendous encouragement, helpful insights, and practical support.

Jim Boyle coordinated and assisted with a feasibility study that validated my approach to post-traumatic stress. Lewis Messinger arranged many interviews and opportunities to survey troops. Ken Sampson, Ken Bush, Randy Edwards, and Doug Kinder all provided opportunities to conduct training on the material, which sharpened my focus and resulted in an overall better product.

I am also truly grateful to the Soldiers who shared their stories and completed surveys during my doctoral research so that I would be able to help other servicemembers later with the results of my work. Most of them are not named in the book, and identifiable details are withheld to preserve privacy and anonymity.

I'm grateful to Patricia Radcliffe, who meticulously worked through the early chapters, making helpful corrections and recommendations that resulted in a better and more concise presentation, as well as to Kevin Weaver and his editorial team at the Warrior's Journey (thewarriorsjourney.org), who diligently reviewed this revised manuscript and agreed to republish it.

Lastly and most importantly, I want to thank my wife, Denise, for her steady and unwavering support not only for this book, but also for all my writing projects that have followed. Denise, you are a winner in everyway. I love you.

INTRODUCTION

O Lord, you hear the desire of the afflicted;
*   you will strengthen their heart; you will incline your ear*
to do justice to the fatherless and the oppressed,
*   so that man who is of the earth may strike terror no more.*
                                                      —Psalm 10:17–18

O N June 28, 2008, former Army Specialist Joseph P. Dwyer died of an accidental overdose of drugs at his home in Pinehurst, North Carolina. Dwyer gained notoriety after a *Military Times* photo of him rescuing an injured Iraqi boy appeared around the world.[1] Sadly, Specialist Dwyer, who served as a medic in the 3rd Squadron, 7th Cavalry Regiment, 3rd Infantry Division (Mechanized), also suffered from post-traumatic stress (PTS) and likely post-traumatic stress disorder (PTSD).

For years after leaving the battlefield, Dwyer struggled with the effects of wartime trauma that contributed to marital failure and substance abuse, among other problems. Yet, despite his service, patriotism shown in joining the military after 9/11, and survival of bullets and bombs, Joseph Dwyer ended up another casualty of war—a likely victim of the bloodless wounds of PTSD.

While PTSD is not new, among warriors or among the general public, it was not formally identified as a mental health disorder until 1980. Since the resurgence of interest in PTSD generated by the issues reported among Vietnam veterans (e.g., as reported in *Achilles in Vietnam: Combat Trauma and the Undoing of Character* by Jonathan Shay), the treatment of PTSD in particular and more generally, post-traumatic stress (PTS)*, has been almost solely a clinical or mental health endeavor. But the trauma that leads to PTS while it has clinical symptoms or effects that warrant clinical intervention, also often has a profound spiritual dimension that requires spiritual intervention. In other words, clergy have an important role to play in the treatment of those who suffer from PTS and who exhibit the symptoms of spiritual trauma.

What many veterans experience in war often continues within them after war, symptoms raging in their souls. Erich Maria Remarque describes it in his novel *The Road Back* as "a still, silent war [that] has ravaged this country of my memories."[2] It is a war that persists, a silent, ongoing re-experiencing phenomenon that manifests in a variety of psychological, physiological, and spiritual symptoms. It is an invisible wounding of the heart and soul that may include such symptoms as: intrusive thoughts, nightmares, sleeplessness, emotional numbness, depression, anger, hypervigilance, a sense

---

* I will use this general term, post-traumatic stress, to also include what is clinically understood as PTSD.

of meaninglessness, grief, guilt, shame, and loss of faith, as well as many other losses. They express themselves in various ways, such as in spiritual dissonance about suffering, trust issues, theological questions about the source of evil, survivor's guilt, and the search for meaning, forgiveness, and reconciliation. Severe symptoms may lead to spiritual disconnection or having a sense of being lost.

The extent of combat exposure is a significant factor when measuring the effects of war. Generally, the greater one's exposure to combat or the more intense the combat trauma, the more likely a person develops PTS later. Other factors include the service-member's background, life experiences, existence of previous trauma, level of training, spiritual perspective, and degree of connection with others. The presence of these factors affects the development of PTS symptoms. But anyone, given enough exposure to trauma over time, will develop symptoms of PTS. For example, many soldiers engaged in the trench warfare of the First World War eventually broke down to some degree and manifested symptoms of PTS, some acutely and some chronically, resulting in years of suffering and dysfunction.

The presence of PTS symptoms is widely evident today in our veteran community. In interviews I conducted with thirty Operation Iraqi Freedom (OIF) and Operation Enduring Freedom (OEF) veterans, almost all of them reported PTS, some symptoms only manifesting many months after the traumatic event(s).

In both world wars and the Korean conflict, the number of psychological casualties exhibiting PTS was greater than the number of those who were killed in combat. And the chances of becoming a psychological casualty in those wars were greater than the chances of being killed by the enemy. (In Vietnam, the chances were about equal.[3]) So there is no doubt that many veterans in our communities struggle with the effects of war-related trauma. While symptoms fade over time, many remain like open wounds, evidence of deep and abiding pain.

The Vietnam War produced thousands of psycho-spiritual casualties.[4] Specific incidences of PTSD among Vietnam veterans are comparable to that among World War II veterans. In studies of Vietnam veterans who served in combat, researchers observed a strong relationship between PTS and other adjustment problems. Similar problems are observed among veterans returning from the wars in Iraq and Afghanistan today.

Soldiers suffering from PTS typically experience adjustment problems and relational issues, such as marital and work challenges. Most of the combat veterans I've counseled over the years indicated problems with their marriages, adjustments problems at home, conflicts at work or with family, and general inability to fit in with society. Regardless of the war—Vietnam, Iraq, or Afghanistan—the effects are mostly the same.

Spiritual trauma or injury shatters a person's perception of the world—assumptions about how things are supposed to be or about how things should work. The experience undermines the victim's sense of security. Trauma assaults a person's sense of justice, rationality, morality, and identity, raising a whole host of questions and doubts that represent spiritual injury.

We can effectively address spiritual injuries by making spiritual interventions, applying Christian principles and biblical resources through cognitive reappraisals. The sufferer's perspective of her or his trauma can be reframed in a way that accounts for the trauma. Only then will the person find meaning for their trauma and eventually recover so that she or he is able to function again. The Scriptures lend themselves to cognitive interventions because God uses his Word to inform our faith and prompt us to view circumstances differently. The importance of God's Word, coupled with faith and the presence of the Holy Spirit, should not be underestimated. But cognitive reappraisal is much more than applying Scripture, saying a prayer, or reading a Bible verse.

Some research suggests leveraging spirituality-based approaches with veterans may even be more effective than traditional clinical approaches.[5] The experience of trauma and its subsequent effects present numerous existential concerns that require thoughtful and theological responses. Most clinicians are not qualified to address these concerns, but many pastoral caregivers do possess the qualifications. Moreover, given the opportunity to understand the nature of trauma and its effects, pastoral caregivers can make appropriate interventions. My studies indicate that combat veterans who explored their trauma through the lens of spirituality were able to find peace. Such peace set them free from their personal prisons and facilitated healing, renewal, and even growth. Many of them discovered God's love covers a multitude of sins, and through the knowledge of God's truth, they found forgiveness, hope, and reconciliation.

This book is about those types of interventions: interventions that address the spiritual dimension of trauma and provide for the possibility of healing among those who suffer most from the enduring effects of their trauma, whether war-related or related to some other type of experience.

We learn the most about suffering when we consider the suffering of Christ. His suffering not only brought about spiritual healing and reconciliation but serves as a paradigm for understanding all trauma and suffering. Having an understanding of Christ's passion enables victims of trauma to view their trauma differently. It helps them discover meaning in their suffering by coming to a realization of the meaning of Christ's suffering.

The first half of this book will give you an overview, focusing on the nature of trauma and its effects. It examines trauma's effects with an emphasis on the spiritual dimension, and suggests many of the so-called clinical effects, such as sleeplessness, withdrawal, and anger, are often manifestations of deeper, spiritual issues. Such issues may be known by the sufferer or remain below the surface of consciousness.

In chapters 1 and 2, we consider the nature of trauma, the spiritual dimension of trauma, PTS and PTSD, spiritual coping, and the effects of trauma from both a negative and positive standpoint. We'll also look at information on spirituality in the treatment of PTS and conclude with guidelines for pastoral caregivers, a discussion about effective practices, and the communalization of trauma.

Chapters 3 and 4 are devoted to a discussion of grief and loss. While grief is a universal experience, the nature of grief for veterans is somewhat different, particularly as it relates to various forms of loss. Often associated with grief are problems of anger and depression, typical symptoms of PTS.

Chapter 5 addresses guilt and shame, which are significant issues for veterans suffering with PTS, especially survivor's guilt.

Chapter 6 marks the second half of the book and explores the remedies for guilt and shame, with a discussion of confession and forgiveness from a biblical perspective.

Chapter 7 explores the problem of evil and suffering. Clergy who expect to effectively assist the sufferer must possess a useful theology of suffering and evil, and be capable of guiding the sufferer through the maze of concerns presented by this problem and of meeting their challenge to find meaning in suffering.

Chapter 8 explains the theory behind the application of cognitive reconstruction and reframing, which is critical for applying the principles derived from biblical models for healing that are examined in the later chapters.

Chapters 9 and 10 illustrate the reframing concept by examining the suffering of Christ and other biblical models for healing, illustrated in the stories of Job, David, and Paul. Also, I expand on the subject of suffering by developing Paul's concept of suffering.

Chapters 11 and 12 discuss resilience, spirituality, and post-traumatic growth. Victims of trauma don't need to be defined by what happened to them. While trauma changes us, we do not need to be trapped by its negative effects. We can derive strength from what gives us stress, and we can develop resilience by inoculating ourselves against stress.

Notes

1. Kelly Kennedy, "Medic in Famous Photo Dies After PTSD Struggle," *Army Times*, July 3, 2008, accessed December 23, 2015, http://archive.armytimes.com/article/20080703/NEWS/807030320/Medic-famous-photo-dies-after-PTSD-struggle/; Joe Gould, "Spc Joseph Patrick Dwyer, You are Not Forgotten," *Army Times*, October 1, 2012, accessed December 23, 2015, http://outside-thewire.armytimes.com/2012/10/01/spc-joseph-patrick-dwyer-you-are-not-forgotten/.

2. Erich M. Remarque, *The Road Back*, trans. A.W. Wheen (Boston: Little, Brown, 1930), 193.

3. Dave Grossman and Loren Christensen, *On Combat: The Psychology and Physiology of Deadly Conflict in War and Peace*, 2nd ed. (Belleville, IL: PPCT Research Publications, 2007), 11.

4. Donald Meichenbaum, *A Clinical Handbook/Practical Therapist Manual for Assessing and Treating Adults with Post-traumatic Stress Disorder (PTSD)* (Waterloo, Ontario: Institute Press, 1994); Grossman and Christensen, *On Combat*.

5. Kenneth Pargament, Gina Magyar-Russell, and Nichole A. Murray-Swank, "The Sacred and the Search for Significance: Religion as a Unique Process," *Journal of Social Issues* 61, no. 4 (2005): 665–687; Larry Dewey, *War and Redemption: Treatment and Recovery in Combat-related Post-traumatic Stress Disorder* (Burlington, VT: Ashgate Publishing, 2004); Andrew J. Weaver, Laura T. Flannelly, James Garbarino, Charles R. Figley & Kevin J. Flannelly, "A Systematic Review of Research on Religion and Spirituality in the *Journal of Traumatic Stress*: 1990-1999," *Mental Health, Religion & Culture* 6, no. 3 (2003): 215-228.

CHAPTER 1

TRAUMA AND POST-TRAUMA STRESS EFFECTS

PTSD is a whole-body tragedy, an integral human event of enormous proportions with massive repercussions.

—Susan Pease Banitt, LCSW

WARTIME trauma produces profound psychological, physiological, and spiritual effects. While not everyone who goes to war returns damaged, all are affected, and many veterans are suffering today with the symptoms of post-traumatic stress. The differences between PTS and PTSD have to do with the extent and duration of the symptoms and whether the symptomology meets the clinical criteria for a diagnosis of PTSD. Again, for our purposes, references to PTS may also include clinical symptoms that would be descriptive of PTSD.

In this chapter, we consider the wide range of effects of combat-related trauma, laying a foundation for understanding the spiritual aspects of trauma and the necessity for spiritual intervention. When we focus on spiritual aspects, many of the associated effects—whether mental, emotional, or physical—diminish and become manageable.

There is hope, and healing is possible. No one suffering from PTS has to suffer with it forever. This may seem quite radical, but recovery is possible. Veterans can get their lives back and find healing through the use of spiritual interventions. But before I get to all of that, we need to understand the nature of trauma and how it affects our servicemembers returning from combat.

TRAUMA AND PTSD

Amazingly, nearly half of all Americans will experience or witness a symptom-producing traumatic event in their lifetime, such as a violent death, sexual assault, or natural disaster.[1] While many Americans adjust quickly to their traumatic experiences, some do not. Most people who are traumatized experience some impairment immediately following the event; they may experience insomnia, nightmares, or disturbing thoughts and memories. In most cases, depending upon the trauma and how the particular person views the trauma, symptoms eventually go away within a few months.

However, in cases where people find impairment of their everyday functioning lasting for at least a month, there is the likelihood they are suffering from the effects associated with the onset of PTSD.[2]

Combat-related trauma is just one type of trauma that may result in PTS or eventually lead to PTSD. While hundreds of thousands of veterans suffer from PTS, many more do not exhibit any debilitating symptoms as a result of their wartime experiences. Nevertheless, PTS is a significant issue in our veteran community, and many veterans suffer with its symptoms.

Combat-Related PTSD

The combat environment is hostile, unpredictable, and emotionally traumatic because of the fear of the unknown. Servicemembers are subject to multiple scenarios, from the possibility of being wounded or killed to engaging the enemy or witnessing a horrific incident. Whether a servicemember experiences one traumatic episode or is exposed to a series of traumas over time, the effects can be devastating.

In 2007, researchers from the Walter Reed Army Institute of Research (WRAIR) reported 10–15 percent of Soldiers developed PTSD after deployment to Iraq, while 11 percent developed PTSD after service in Afghanistan.[3] It is estimated that somewhere between 13 and 20 percent of servicemembers are suffering with PTSD.[4] But the actual percentage of servicemembers suffering with PTSD may be much higher.[5]

According to records of the Defense Manpower Data Center, as of May 2012, 1,515,707 veterans of Operation Enduring Freedom (OEF), Operation Iraqi Freedom (OIF), and Operation New Dawn (OND) have separated from the military.[6] This number includes servicemembers who died in-theater. If 15 percent of these servicemembers have PTSD, then well over 200,000 veterans from these wars may be suffering from PTSD.

According to a Veterans Affairs (VA) report that assessed veterans who served in OEF, OIF, and OND from the first quarter of fiscal year 2002 through the third quarter of fiscal year 2012, nearly 30 percent of its patients from Iraq and Afghanistan have PTSD.[7] As of 2012, the VA had in total treated over 830,000 veterans from these wars. This means at least 249,000 veterans treated at VA hospitals and clinics have been diagnosed with PTSD. The figure is astounding, given the likelihood that there are many more veterans who suffer with PTSD from other wars or have never been seen by the VA.[8]

ASSOCIATED PROBLEMS

There are many problems associated with PTSD, particularly anxiety, depression, and suicide. Of the 13 to 20 percent of veterans overall who suffer with PTSD, 10 percent also suffer from an anxiety disorder, which highlights the challenges of those diagnosed with PTSD. Additionally, some studies further report that 35–75 percent of those suffering with PTSD suffer with depression.

There is no doubt that anxiety and depression contribute to the high number of marital difficulties among veterans diagnosed with PTSD. These difficulties manifest in terms of self-disclosure, intimacy, expressiveness, and aggression.[9]

Nearly 20 percent of those who suffer with PTSD, unfortunately, will also attempt suicide.[10] Suicide has steadily increased in all the military services since 2002. There was a marked increase in the occurrence of suicides among combat troops after 2005. This increase correlates with the surge of troops in Iraq that began in 2005. Additionally, some standards for enlistment in the Army were waived around 2005, and this resulted in the recruitment of individuals with a wide range of preexisting conditions that may have contributed to the increase in suicides.

In 2012, 349 servicemembers took their own lives. Indeed, there were more servicemembers who died by their own hands in 2012 than those who died in combat—and more than one-third of those who took their lives in 2012 had never been deployed.[11] But while the number of suicides in the military increases, its documented connection to combat-related PTSD is less clear. Nevertheless, there is a connection between PTSD and suicide, and veterans who suffer from the chronic effects of PTSD are at risk for suicide.

TRAUMA

What is trauma? The term *trauma* originates from ancient Greek and means to wound or to hurt.[12] Trauma involves a significant crisis and is connected to a deeply disturbing and disruptive event that causes great distress, often attended by shock and fear. It frequently involves physical, moral, spiritual, and psychological injury. Trauma, then, is a wounding, and in many instances a wounding of the heart and soul.

Post-trauma stress is typically negative stress or distress, which causes dysfunction. However, while trauma is hurtful and stressful, not all stress is bad, and not all trauma is completely negative or results in dysfunction.

The experience of trauma may challenge someone's worldview and assumptions about life, i.e., how he or she assumes the world operates or expects things to turn out. The occurrence of trauma is often a life-changing event that rocks a person's world; it taxes and overwhelms one's capability to adapt or resume normal functioning. This latter aspect is always associated with a disorder, and PTSD is evident when there is a disruption of normal functioning that results in overall dysfunction and distress.

Violent events that threaten well-being, such as what one might expect in combat or from natural disasters, confront individuals at the limits of their capabilities. These events sometime evoke a catastrophic response.[13] That response often contributes to PTS.

PHYSIOLOGICAL IMPACT

Besides the emotional, mental, or spiritual effects, trauma produces many physiological effects. Trauma affects the body's "flight or fight" response, which impacts the nervous system and engages the cardiovascular, respiratory, and gastrointestinal systems. It is common for a warrior to lose bladder and bowel control, hyperventilate, or physically freeze due to fear while engaged in intense combat operations. In a government study that evaluated the performance of Soldiers in World War II, cited by Lieutenant Colonel Dave Grossman in his book *On Combat: The Psychology and Physiology of Deadly Conflict in War and Peace*, researchers concluded that one-quarter of all U.S. troops admitted they had lost control of their bladder, and an eighth of them also admitted to loss of bowel control.[14]

Traumatic stress impacts the nervous system, particularly the sympathetic nervous system (SNS) and the parasympathetic nervous system (PNS). Both are part of the autonomic nervous system (ANS), which is hard-wired to an area of the brain called the limbic system.[15] This part of the brain stores memories of life-threatening events. A brief discussion of the ANS is helpful here because it will not only explain the effects of stress on the body but also help us understand how PTSD can develop later.

The ANS comprises three parts: the SNS and PNS mentioned above, and the enteric nervous system (ENS). The ANS regulates the functions of the body's internal organs and is always "on duty" to maintain normal equilibrium—what is called *homeostasis*.[16] The ANS controls smooth muscles such as those in the eye and around blood vessels, hair follicles, the bladder, and intestines. It regulates glandular secretions, heart rate, respiration, and the stomach. It accounts for why hair stands on end when one is frightened or nervous, why a person experiences dry mouth, and why some people sweat profusely under duress. The ANS is not something that we consciously think about because it functions involuntarily.

The ANS activates the "flight or fight" response during emergency situations. When stimulated, the SNS is responsible for releasing two primary chemicals, noradrenaline and adrenaline, resulting in physiological changes that include pupil dilation, increased heart rate, rise in blood pressure, and increased sweating. The focus of the SNS is survival. The primary emotion associated with this response is anger.

The PNS activates the rest mode during nonemergencies. The PNS and SNS work in opposition to each other in order to contribute to homeostasis. Generally, when the body is in a rest mode, the PNS allows it to recover and relax.

The ENS consists of a complex network of nerves that primarily monitors the digestive system. Sometimes it is referred to as the "gut brain." When stimulated in connection with the other parts of the ANS, the ENS accounts for an array of responses, including diarrhea when a person is frightened and stomach cramping when the body is stressed.

Each system performs its role. For example, suppose Sergeant Smith, a member of a team, is conducting routine operations in what has been a quiet sector of the Helmand Province in Afghanistan. He is now returning to his base. His PNS has moved into a "rest and recoup" mode, conserving energy by lowering his heart rate and aiding digestion.

Suddenly there is an explosion, and then another explosion and the clatter of small arms fire. His vehicle has been attacked. Sergeant Smith's PNS reacts to his SNS, which is increasing his blood pressure, raising his heart rate, and reducing his digestion. All of this is occurring without any conscious thought on the part of Sergeant Smith.

It is the interaction between these systems that take a toll on the warrior. The attack on Sergeant Smith's vehicle results in profound physiological changes and a massive expenditure of emotional and physical energy. Then the attack is over and he is back at his base, in relative safety. His team survived the attack and repelled the enemy. What happens next? His PNS activates to compensate for the massive energy release. The system lowers the heart rate, reduces respiration and blood pressure, and opens the bowels. This is sometimes referred to as "parasympathetic backlash." His body goes into maintenance mode.

Sergeant Smith and his team are exhausted and need sleep. They burned a lot of adrenaline and must get rest. But suppose they cannot rest? Perhaps there is another mission? Continued operations will tax them, winding them tightly like a coiled spring. Erratic or continued tension will induce a temporary hormonal high but eventually result in a combat stress reaction that could lead to PTSD later.

Without the necessary downtime, the team is unable to physically recover. The body cannot remain in a constant state of vigilance without an effect—usually problems with sleep and anger later on, two very common symptoms of PTSD. The experience of the hormonal high, an adrenaline kick, is like the high of an addictive drug. It may explain why some servicemembers returning from combat are unable to adjust to the boredom of noncombat operations and civilian life.

These physiological effects are factors in the development of fatigue, detachment, isolation, and apathy. They explain why some servicemembers have problems with sleep or irritability and, in worse cases, anger and rage. They account for poor concentration and memory loss after servicemembers return home. Constant vigilance coupled with persistent sleep deprivation affects the neurological system. It is a physiological reason for the persistence of these problems when a warfighter returns home. Caregivers can help warfighters by making them aware of this problem. Understanding it may help them realize that there are physical and fairly normal reasons why they are responding in this way.

The inevitability of these effects is one reason the military pulls warfighters periodically out of the fight for a brief time-out. Periodic rest and recuperation from combat not only sustains the warrior, but lessens the likelihood of long-term effects from these physiological realities.[17]

Emotional and Psychological Reactions

Trauma also produces profound emotional and psychological reactions. A traumatic event may trigger painful experiences from the past. Often, servicemembers suffering with PTSD succumb to re-experiencing the originating trauma through trigger events such as a sight, a smell, or a sound. These events provoke vivid memories and result in re-traumatization.

Several Soldiers have related to me how a pile of trash on the side of a road triggered emotional reactions in them. In Iraq or Afghanistan, it was common for the enemy to hide improvised explosive devices (IEDs) in piles of trash. The sight of civilians in Muslim dress may elicit reactions because the enemy sometimes concealed explosives under their garments. I recall flinching while passing under bridges that were occupied, because the enemy was known to throw grenades from overpasses at passing vehicles. Sometimes you see a veteran duck or flinch at the sound of a siren. That's because sirens were used to alert warfighters of impending attacks in the combat zone. Such reactions in combat were a matter of survival, but back home they might seem strange or foolish.

A traumatic event may be attended by feelings of disgust, shame, and wrongness—feelings typical among victims of sexual assault. The sense of wrongness may stem from a personal violation or error. Incidences of rape occur in the combat zone, and some warfighters are traumatized not because of combat but because of such personal violations.[18] I have counseled Soldiers and am aware of others whose traumatic experiences were the result of dysfunction in units, poor treatment by others, inferior leadership, or betrayal. These types of incidents and their effects are sometimes characterized as *moral injuries*.

Some servicemembers suffer from a sudden realization of the unfairness of life as it affects other servicemembers. The arbitrary loss of life, in which one warfighter dies and another lives, perhaps as the result of a rocket that just happens to strike a living area, seems unjust and senseless. This perception of meaninglessness contributes to PTS and is often a symptom of it.

Radical and Positive Transformation

Trauma may result in radical and positive transformation.[19] Later I will consider some of these positive reactions. Although numerous studies and anecdotal evidence point to positive outcomes, how a person responds to trauma always depends upon that person's appraisal of the event. What might be traumatic and negative for one person might not be traumatic to someone else. A third person might even construe that experience as something positive.

Spiritual Aspects of Trauma

There are many spiritual aspects to trauma. Trauma sometimes disrupts a person's ability to understand, predict, or control one's life. There can be a disruption of a person's spiritual values, which may include beliefs, practices, and relationships among other aspects.[20] This kind of disruption has devastating effects, resulting in the inability to cope with the normal requirements of living. In these instances, the traumatic event not only affects a person's core beliefs or values but assumptions about the world and how he or she thinks it should work. All of these aspects may be described as spiritual trauma.

Spiritual trauma is an assault on a person's sense of security, self-image, and the way he or she usually derives meaning in life. It is not difficult to comprehend, then, how combat traumas or personal violations might contribute to a breakdown in normal expectations and assumptions. This aspect of trauma is significant and requires our examination. In the next chapter, we'll look at the spiritual dimension of trauma in greater detail, and in subsequent chapters consider specific examples of spiritual trauma. Then we'll consider how appropriate spiritual interventions can effectively address these issues.

Moral Injury v. Spiritual Injury

Moral injury or moral trauma is the result or the aftermath of experiencing severe trauma, witnessing horrible things that are incongruent with a person's values, or participating in actions or observing events that transgress sincerely held beliefs and expectations. It is a secondary injury resulting from the experience of an originating trauma. It is the act of transgression that is particularly egregious and contributes mostly to moral traumatization regardless if those beliefs or expectations are rooted in spiritual beliefs.[21]

These persons are also usually spiritually injured or distressed because many sincerely held beliefs are typically grounded in religion or spirituality. Combat-related moral injury stems from participating in killing, violating beliefs that are in conflict with orders, or simply observing the horror of war such as the death of innocent civilians, fellow comrades, and even the death of enemy combatants.

Moral and spiritual injuries are not the same as PTS or PTSD but they represent symptoms that are often concomitant with a diagnosis of PTS/D. Furthermore, moral and spiritual injuries, while similar in manifestation, are not exactly the same. Moral injury presents as a violation of conscience or betrayal or the transgression of deeply held beliefs and expectations. Such beliefs may be religious, cultural, social or personal. Spiritual injury may be viewed similarly but the critical difference is that there's injury to one's spirituality. Spirituality is a broad concept that has to do with the way a person understands the world or perceives the Transcendent. People are spiritual beings and their spirituality may be derived from some moral code, religious teaching, or sense of meaning. Spirituality is about how people connect with others or pursue ideals that are larger than self. Spiritual trauma is an assault on one's sense of spirituality, assumptions about how the world operates or the way he or she derives meaning in life.

In my view spiritual and moral injuries overlap, but spiritual injuries include the effects of trauma upon the heart, soul, and human spirit. Spiritually injured servicemembers are broken souls, persons who've lost their sense of direction and purpose in life or their faith or hope as a result of some significant traumatic event(s) in combat.

Moral injury, like spiritual injury, has emotional and behavioral consequences. People who are injured in this way may feel ashamed or worthless. They may feel guilty and not worthy of forgiveness— from others, themselves, or God. Guilt manifests in a variety of ways: as survivor's guilt—*I lived but my friend died*, false guilt—*I should have died instead*, or justified guilt—*I killed the prisoner*.

Anger is often present regardless if it is related to a perceived moral or spiritual injury. As a perceived spiritual injury, it may be anger directed at God. As a perceived moral injury, it may be anger related to betrayal. Servicemembers may be angry over leadership lapses or the loss of friends; however, they also may be angry with God, feeling that he let them down or worse, betrayed them too. Self-blame or complicated grief has moral connections, but they also have spiritual ties. Given the interrelationship between moral and spiritual injury, these injuries may be seen together and treated similarly.

PTSD

In the United States PTSD is fairly common with approximately 6–8 percent of the adult population meeting the strict criteria for a diagnosis.[22] Likely, there are many more who suffer from a range of PTS symptoms but do not meet the clinical criteria for PTSD. As the fifth most common "mental illness," PTSD currently afflicts as many as 5.2 million Americans between the ages of eighteen and fifty-four.[23]

In the United States PTSD is often the result of sexual assault or domestic violence. Human-induced trauma is the most troubling form of trauma, whether it is assault or combat related. Interpersonal human aggression is the universal fear. This is because it is more difficult to assign meaning to human aggression than to other forms of trauma, such as natural disasters. This fact contributes most to the problem of PTSD.[24]

But what exactly is PTSD and how does it manifest? PTSD is a delayed reaction to a traumatic event or a series of traumatic events, in which an array of symptoms persists for at least a month.[25] It is evident in people when it disrupts normal functioning. Symptoms may show up several months or even years after a traumatic event(s). It is important to remember that PTSD is a normal reaction to an abnormal situation or extraordinary event(s).

The hallmark feature of PTSD is the intrusive re-experiencing of an originating trauma. Like an irritating tune that keeps playing in your head, the originating trauma—often triggered by a sight, sound, or smell—is replayed over and over again. Sufferers become stuck in the pain of the original trauma. Often deprived of sleep, they feel trapped, held captive by the power of the trauma.

The Spanish referred to PTSD as *estar roto*, which means, "to be broken."[26] This is quite appropriate because many people who suffer with PTSD experience significant impairment of personal, social, and occupational functions. They feel their lives are broken; indeed, many of them are broken souls. They often experience anguish accompanied by deep anxiety because they cannot seem to return to being the people they were before.

Not all trauma leads to the development of PTSD. But PTSD is always the result of trauma. The development of combat-related PTSD correlates with several factors: the degree of trauma in war (intensity), proximity to the trauma (range), extent of exposure (duration), and frequency of traumatic experiences.

In truth, no one is immune from PTSD. Statistics from three wars confirm this observation. There were more PTS-related casualties from World War I, World War II, and the Korean War combined than casualties who were killed or physically wounded.[27]

Not all stress casualties resulted in PTSD, but significant numbers of servicemembers did exhibit post-traumatic stress. Others developed PTSD and some eventually learned to manage their symptoms and recovered. Servicemembers may lessen their risk of developing PTSD through training, resiliency-building measures, and other factors such as faith. Warfighters properly trained and positively oriented are less likely to develop PTSD or chronically suffer from the long-term effects of PTSD.

PTSD and Other Combat Stress Reactions

Combat-related PTSD usually results from losses (such as the deaths of fellow servicemembers) or from guilt associated with perceived or actual failure. It can be the result of witnessing the horrors of war, such as killings, mutilations, civilian deaths, atrocities, or betrayal. Other circumstances also contribute to the development of PTSD in servicemembers, and many of these will be explored in the chapters that follow.

Because every person is different, the response to a traumatic event depends on the individual. The different kinds of responses people may have to trauma range from combat stress or "battle fatigue" to chronic PTSD. Chronic PTSD is a severe and lasting reaction to a traumatic event. Chronic PTSD may manifest initially as acute stress disorder or acute PTSD. The difference between the two has to do with the duration of the symptoms, their extent, and when they manifest. It is the chronic form that is most debilitating.[28]

Combat operational stress reactions (COSRs) are common and may include sleeplessness, eating problems, intrusive thoughts, hyperalertness, and other, similar reactions, which usually go away within three months.[29]

In contrast to typical COSRs, PTSD is the most severe of all stress reactions and includes the re-experiencing or chronic intrusiveness of a traumatic event. The sufferer may act or feel like the event is happening again, experience nightmares, or react with acute sensory alertness, such as jumping at the sound of a siren or a car backfiring. Servicemembers who report PTSD symptoms may also indicate numbness—an inability to attach to someone emotionally or relationally—and avoidance of places, people, activities, or events because of their association with the traumatic experience.[30]

SYMPTOMS OF PTSD

The *Diagnostic and Statistical Manual of Mental Disorders*, fifth edition (DSM-5) describes PTSD as a trauma and stressor-related disorder.[31] In the earlier edition of the DSM, PTSD was listed as an anxiety disorder.[32] The DSM-5 identifies six criteria for a diagnosis of PTSD and includes several significant changes from the previous edition.

The clinical definition of PTSD is complex, suggesting it is not particularly easy to be diagnosed with PTSD. But many service-members and veterans manifest various symptoms of post-traumatic stress, and while they may not be clinically eligible for a diagnosis of PTSD, they have symptoms that warrant intervention. While it is not the clergy's task to diagnose symptoms, they can intervene. Learning how to intervene on a spiritual basis is what this book is all about.

THE CLINICAL CRITERIA FOR PTSD[33]

- *Criterion A: Exposure to Trauma or a Major Stressor.* According to the DSM-5, the criteria for determining a clinical diagnosis of PTSD presuppose an exposure to trauma, defined as a violent or accidental event occurring outside the person, either witnessed or experienced through repeated or extreme exposure to negative details.

- *Criterion B: Presence of Intrusion Symptoms.* (Only *one* of the following is required.) There must be the presence of recurring intrusion symptoms after the event(s) that manifest as (1) distressing memories; (2) intrusive dreams or nightmares (in severe cases, flashbacks in which the person feels or acts as if the traumatic event was actually happening again); and (3) intense or prolonged distress.

- *Criterion C: Persistent Avoidance of Stimuli.* These stimuli are associated with the traumatic event(s), beginning after the traumatic event(s) occurred, as evidenced by one or both of the following (only *one* of the following is required): (1) avoidance of distressing memories, thoughts, or feelings about the trauma and (2) avoidance of external reminders (people, places, conversations, activities, objects, situations) that arouse distressing memories, thoughts, or feelings about or closely associated with the traumatic events(s).

- *Criterion D: Negative Alterations in Thoughts and Mood.* The alterations begin or worsen after the event(s) (*two* of the following are required): (1) An inability to remember key features of the event; (2) persistent negative or exaggerated beliefs or expectations about oneself or the world; (3) persistent distorted thoughts about the cause or consequences of the event(s), such as blaming self or others; (4) persistent negative emotional state (e.g., fear, horror, anger, guilt, or shame); (5) markedly diminished interest or participation in pre-traumatic significant activities; (6) feelings of detachment or estrangement from others; and (7) persistent inability to experience positive emotions (e.g., happiness, satisfaction, or loving feelings).

- *Criterion E: Marked Alterations in Arousal and Reactivity.* The alterations are associated with the traumatic event(s), beginning or worsening after the traumatic event(s) occurred (at least *two* of the following are required): (1) irritable behavior, angry outbursts, aggressive behavior; (2) reckless or self-destructive behavior; (3) hypervigilance; (4) exaggerated startle response; (5) problems with concentration; or (6) sleep disturbance.

Types of Combat Stress Reactions (COSRs)

- Acute Stress Reactions/Combat Stress Reactions equals Trauma exposure plus symptoms lasting 2 to 4 days.
- Acute Stress Disorder (ASD) equals Trauma plus symptoms lasting 4 days to 1 month.
- *Acute PTSD equals symptoms lasting at least 1 month but less than 3 months.
- Chronic PTSD equals symptoms lasting more than 3 months after the traumatic event.

The real issue with exhibiting symptoms of PTSD is when it manifests chronically, persisting longer than a month.

Figure 1.1: Types of Combat Stress Reactions

- *Criterion F: Duration.* The duration of the disturbances listed in criteria B, C, D, and E persists longer than one month. The disturbance caused by the trauma must result in significant distress or impairment in social, occupational, or other important areas of functioning. In special cases, a diagnosis must specify when dissociative symptoms are present (numbing, depersonalization, or derealization, in which the person feels numb, feels outside of themselves, or has a sense that things are not real), or when the disturbance is not due to drugs or other illness. Preliminary diagnosis may be given as early as one month after the event, but a full diagnosis is not met until at least six months after the traumatic experience(s).

Regardless of the type of traumatic event, a traumatic event does not necessarily result in PTSD nor does it result exclusively in PTSD. It is normal to be affected by trauma.

Guiding Principles for Treatment

There is no one preferred treatment for PTSD or evidence that any treatment is vastly superior to another. However, there are treatment principles that apply regardless of the methodology employed.

In this book, you will learn how to intervene through a methodology called *cognitive restructuring*. Two aspects of cognitive restructuring are *narrative reconstruction* and *narrative reframing*. I thoroughly explain them later on and then illustrate them using biblical examples. My approach uses principles found in cognitive-behavioral therapy (CBT).[34] CBT involves working with the victim's cognitions in order to change the way the victim thinks, feels, and acts in relation to the traumatic experience. The use of corrective feedback, new information, and counterargument are several ways cognitive restructuring occurs. Therefore, CBT is particularly effective in attribution retraining and changing feelings of shame and guilt by teaching the sufferer how to reframe perceptions of the trauma, leading to a new perspective and healing.

So what are some of the principles we should use in treatment? Below are five significant guiding principles that I feel are essential for treatment.

- Use a Client-Centered Approach

  A client-centered approach focuses on the needs of the veteran and begins where the client is; nothing is forced and no demands are placed on the client. The veteran participates in the development and application of the treatment. This approach to treatment grants some personal control to the client and gives discretion to him or her over what is shared, how it is shared, and when it is shared. Voluntary involvement is critical. No one should be coerced, especially when spiritual protocols are being used. In the program I use, warfighters must begin together;

27

no one may be added to the group after group treatment begins. But members may leave the group during treatment if they choose. Should they decide later to seek treatment, they need to join a newly formed group.

- **Lead Them to Meaning**
  Encourage self-discovery. Let the victim "connect the dots" that lead to the discovery of meaning. People who find meaning in their suffering find healing. Treatment requires sufferers to sever their connections to the past traumatic event and replace painful memories or emotions associated with that event with newly conditioned emotional responses and/or new cognitive constructs that provide relief.[35] Healing begins when victims learn to separate the memory of the experience from the pain. Successful treatment enables the veteran/victim to live constructively in the present.

- **Conduct a Full Assessment**
  It is essential for those who provide treatment to conduct a full assessment of those who come into their care, taking into consideration associated problems and presenting issues, especially if these issues might present obstacles in exploring the trauma itself. Client-centered approaches emphasize the need for practitioners to allow clients to open the doors into their own souls. Prying at someone's trauma, especially if there are layers of protective coping, may completely shut the person down, or worse, retraumatize the person unnecessarily. Effective treatment plans also address multiple factors, including medical, relational, psychological, vocational, and spiritual factors. The practitioner must help separate the victim from the trauma

and educate them about the nature of PTSD. As much as possible, caregivers should try to normalize the traumatic effect by contextualizing it or helping the sufferer to see the problem objectively. Finally, since most pastoral caregivers are not qualified to make a diagnosis of PTSD, don't diagnose. Deal with the presenting symptoms. If referral to a clinician is necessary, then do so. Keep in mind that there are clinical issues as well as spiritual issues. Only clinicians are qualified to address the clinical symptoms of PTSD.

- **Create a Safe Environment**
  Providing treatment in a safe environment where relationships are based on trust and compassion is essential. This is achieved when the practitioner establishes client-counselor rapport, identifies and adheres to ground rules, and honors the client's needs. Many pastoral caregivers, especially military chaplains, have the experience, skills, and rapport to conduct group sessions that provide for a servicemember's safety and expression of painful experiences. Just the verbal expression of pain often reduces it. Establishing rapport in a safe and secure setting is absolutely essential and contributes to a healing alliance.

- **Employ Group Methodology**
  Group treatment is an ideal methodology and widely regarded as essential in any kind of treatment plan. It must be conducted in a safe environment. Conducted properly, it promotes cohesion and mutual support among empathetic members.[36] The use of group methodology facilitates sharing, promotes understanding, exercises patience, expresses empathy, and affirms all members in the group.[37] In a group setting, veterans are

29

comfortable sharing their pain, so long as they feel secure and are confident that trust has been established. This methodology is self-empowering and conducive to healing.

NOTES

1. Matthew J. Friedman, *Post-traumatic and Acute Stress Disorders* 4th ed. (Kansas City: Compact Clinicals, 2006).

2. *Diagnostic and Statistical Manual of Mental Disorders*, 5th ed. (Washington, DC: American Psychiatric Association, 2013)

3. Charles W. Hoge, Carl A. Castro, Stephen C. Messer, Dennis McGurk, Dave I. Cotting, and Robert L. Koffman, "Combat Duty in Iraq and Afghanistan: Mental Health Problems, and Barriers to Care," *New England Journal of Medicine* 351 (2004): 13–22.

4. National Research Council, *Treatment for Posttraumatic Stress Disorder in Military and Veteran Populations: Initial Assessment* (Washington, DC: The National Academies Press, 2012).

5. Jamie Reno, "Nearly 30% of Vets Treated by V.A. Have PTSD," *The Daily Beast*, October 21, 2012, accessed December 23, 2015, www.thedailybeast. com/articles/2012/10/21/nearly-30-of-vets-treated-by-v-a-have-ptsd.html.

6. Epidemiology Program, Post Deployment Health Group, Office of Public Health, Veterans Health Administration, Department of Veterans Affairs. *Report on VA Facility Specific Operation Enduring Freedom (OEF), Operation Iraqi Freedom (OIF), and Operation New Dawn (OND) Veterans Coded with Potential PTSD, from 1st Qtr FY 2002 through 3rd Qtr FY 2012* Washington, DC: Author. Accessed on December 23, 2015. http://www.publichealth.va.gov/epidemiology.

7. Ibid.

8. Ibid.

9. Carl Castro and Jeff Thomas, "The Battlemind Training System" (Arlington, VA: Walter Reed Army Institute of Research, 2007); National Quality Management Program Special Study, *Post-Deployment Post-traumatic Stress Disorder (PTSD) Screening* (Washington, DC: NQMP, January 2006); Michael Lyles, Tim Clinton, and Anthony J. Centore, "Trauma and PTSD: A Clinical Overview," in *Caring for People God's Way: Personal and Emotional Issues, Addictions, Grief, and Trauma*, eds. T. Clinton et al. (Nashville: Thomas Nelson, 2005), 387–408; see www.ptsd.va.gov for articles on the effects of traumatic experiences.

10. Charles W. Hoge, A. Terhakopian, Carl A. Castro, Stephen Messer, and C. C. Engel, "Association of Posttraumatic Stress Disorder with Somatic Symptoms, Health Care Visits, and Absenteeism Among Iraq War Veterans," *The American Journal of Psychiatry* 164 (2007): 150–153; P. Bliese, K. Wright, A. Adler, and J. Thomas, "Validation of the 90 to 120 Day Post-deployment Psychological Short Screen," Walter Reed Army Institute of Research Report #2004-002 (Washington, DC: Author, 2004): 1–11; Matthew J. Friedman, "Acknowledging the Psychiatric Cost of War," *New England Journal of Medicine* 351 (2004): 75–77.

11. J. K. Trotter, "18% More U.S. Troops Committed Suicide Than Died in Combat Last Year," *The Wire*, January 14, 2013, accessed December 23, 2015, www.thewire.com/national/2013/01/us-military-suicides-2012/60985/;

see also Bill Chappell, "US Military Suicide Rate Surpassed Combat Deaths in 2012, " *The Two-Way*, January 14, 2013, accessed December 23, 2015, http://www.npr.org/blogs/thetwo-way/2013/01/14/169364733/u-s-militarys-suicide-rate-surpassed-combat-deaths-in-2012.

12. *American Heritage Dictionary of the English Language*, 4th ed., ed. J.P. Pickett (New York: Houghton Mifflin, 2000), 1836, 2051.

13. Judith Herman, *Trauma and Recovery* (New York: Basic Books, 1992).

14. Grossman and Christensen, *On Combat*, 9; Herman, *Trauma*; Charles W. Hoge, *Once a Warrior Always a Warrior* (Guilford, CT: Lyons Press, 2010).

15. Hoge, *Once a Warrior*.

16. Grossman and Christensen, *On Combat*; Hoge, *Once a Warrior*.

17. Hoge, *Once a Warrior*.

18. Ibid.

19. Lawrence G. Calhoun and Richard G. Tedeschi, "The Foundations of Posttraumatic Growth: An Expanded Framework," in *Handbook of Posttraumatic Growth*, eds. L. G. Calhoun and R. G. Tedeschi (Mahwah, NJ: Lawrence Erlbaum Associates, 2006), 1–23; Annette Mahoney, Elizabeth Krumrei, and Kenneth Pargament, "Broken Vows: Divorce as a Spiritual Trauma and its Implications for Growth and Decline," in *Trauma, Recovery, and Growth: Positive Psychological Perspectives on Posttraumatic Stress*, eds. Stephen Joseph and P. Alex Linley (Hoboken, NJ: Wiley, 2008), 105–123.

20. Mahoney et al., "Broken Vows." See also Robert Grant, "Spirituality and Trauma: An Essay," *Traumatology* 5, no. 1 (1999): 8-10, accessed December 23, 2015, DOI: 10.1177/153476569900500103; M. J. Friedman, Post-traumatic; A. Matsakis, *Post-traumatic Stress Disorder: A Complete Treatment Guide* (Oakland: New Harbinger, 1994).

21. B.T. Litz, N. Stein, N., E. Delaney, L. Lebowitz, W.P. Nash, C. Silva, & S. Maguen, "Moral Injury and Moral Repair in War Veterans: A preliminary model and intervention strategy," *Clinical Psychology Review*, 29 (2009): 695-706.

22. P. Massad and T. Hulsey, "Causal Attributions in Posttraumatic Stress Disorder: Implications for Clinical Research and Practice," *Psychotherapy: Theory, Research, Practice, Training* 43, no. 2 (2006): 201; Committee on the Assessment of Ongoing Efforts in the Treatment of Posttraumatic Stress Disorder, *Treatment for Posttraumatic Stress Disorder in Military and Veteran Populations: Final Assessment* (Washington, DC: National Academies Press, 2014), accessed December 23, 2015, http://www.ncbi.nlm.nih.gov/pubmed/25077185.

23. Lyles et al., "Trauma and PTSD."

24. Grossman and Christensen, *On Combat*; Meichenbaum, *A Clinical Handbook*. See Glenn R. Schiraldi, The Post Traumatic Stress Disorder Source Book (Los Angeles: Lowell House, 2000), 4, 404. Schiraldi cites Schopenhauer who observed, "Suffering which falls to our lot in the course of nature, or by chance, or fate, does not seem so painful as suffering which is inflicted on us by the arbitrary will of another."

25. Aphrodite Matsakis, *Post-traumatic Stress Disorder: A Complete Treatment Guide*; National Center for PTSD Fact Sheet (3) (2007); "Who is Most Likely

to Develop PTSD?" US Department of Veterans Affairs, accessed January 21, 2008, http://www.ncptsd.va.gov/.

26. Edward Tick, *War and the Soul* (Wheaton, IL: Quest Books, 2005).

27. Grossman and Christensen, *On Combat*.

28. *Diagnostic and Statistical Manual of Mental Disorders*, 5th ed.

29. US Army, *Combat and Operational Stress Control for Leaders and Soldiers*, Field Manual (FM) 6-22.5 (Washington, DC: Department of the Army, 2009).

30. Friedman, Post-traumatic; see also A. Matsakis, Post-traumatic; VA/ DoD Clinical Practice Guideline for the Management of Post-Traumatic Stress (2004), US Department of Veterans Affairs, accessed December 23, 2015, http://www.healthquality.va.gov/ptsd/ptsd_full.pdf.

31. *Diagnostic and Statistical Manual of Mental Disorders*, 5th ed.

32. *Diagnostic and Statistical Manual of Mental Disorders*, 4th ed. (Washington, DC: American Psychiatric Association, 2000).

33. Information provided here on the criteria for PTSD is a summary of what is available at http://www.ptsd.va.gov/professional/PTSD-overview/ dsm5_criteria_ptsd.asp and is in the public domain. For a thorough explanation, consult the *Diagnostic and Statistical Manual of Mental Disorders*, 5th ed.

34. Lyles et al., "Trauma and PTSD."

35. Ibid.

36. Lyles et al., "Trauma and PTSD"; S. Bisbey and L. Bisbey, *Brief Therapy for Post-traumatic Stress Disorder: Traumatic Incident Reduction and Related Techniques* (New York: John Wiley, 1998); Meichenbaum, *A Clinical Handbook*; Jonathan Shay, *Achilles in Vietnam: Combat Trauma and the Undoing of Character* (New York: Scribner, 1994).

37. Lyles et al., "Trauma and PTSD"; S. Bisbey and L. Bisbey, *Brief Therapy*.

CHAPTER 2

SPIRITUALITY AND TRAUMA

Every trauma has a spiritual dimension that warrants spiritual intervention.

—Dean Bonura

ADDRESSING the trauma that results in PTS requires an understanding of spirituality. Spirituality is an important concept, and people assign many different meanings to it. We'll briefly consider some of these meanings but not attempt to provide an exhaustive explanation. Coming to some kind of understanding of spirituality is essential in order to grasp the fact that trauma has an inherent spiritual dimension that warrants spiritual intervention.

SPIRITUALITY

The concept of spirituality has to do with the seat of morality and represents the connection one has to the sacred or to the transcendent or to a living and personal God.[1] Spirituality relates to the soul, that which is unique to humanity, the thing that drives us, the essence of life. It contributes to our search for complete integration, balance, and meaning.[2] Spirituality is an all-encompassing, existential concept affecting one's emotions, thoughts, actions, and connections with others.

Everyone has spirituality, but it's manifested differently in each of us. According to Ronald Rolheiser, an authority on contemporary spirituality, it's represented by the concept of *eros*, or desire, and it's how a person channels that desire, either in healthy or unhealthy ways. Spirituality also leads to greater personal integration and connection or to greater disintegration in body, mind, and soul.[3]

Spirituality gives people a way of understanding the world, how it works, how meaning is derived, and how they determine what matters. Spirituality informs a person's assumptions about life; however, spirituality is not the same as religion. Religion is a component of spirituality or an expression of it. While religion may be defined in terms of an institutionalized dogma—a set of tenets, beliefs, or practices that involve traditions and rituals—spirituality is more generally defined, informal, relational, existential, and behavioral.[4]

SPIRITUAL TRAUMA

Trauma affects a victim's spirituality, assumptions about life, and how meaning, purpose, and significance are derived beyond typical social or institutional structures.[5] When one's spirituality is assaulted or disrupted, then those assumptions about life are shaken—or, in some cases, shattered. Ideas about what is good, meaningful, or worthwhile are questioned. This explains why sometimes trauma victims suffer from a crisis of faith: when they feel God is responsible in some way for their trauma or when they blame him for it.

Often those who lose faith in God also lose faith with their religious communities or with their families and friends, and as a result become isolated. These servicemembers feel abandoned by God, conclude that he is irrelevant, or, worse, assume that he betrayed them.

Spiritual trauma is the effect of trauma upon a person's sense of meaning, concept of self, view of God, or understanding of the nature of evil and suffering. Like any aspect of trauma, the extent of spiritual trauma depends on how the traumatic event is perceived by the victim. What is spiritually damaging to one victim may not be damaging to another victim who has gone through the same traumatic experience. The more threatening and damaging the effects of the event on an individual's core spiritual values, the greater the spiritual trauma.

Imagine the symptoms of trauma are like an iceberg, having visible and less visible symptoms. People understand the nature of icebergs: most of their mass is below the surface of the water. What the human eye sees is only the "tip of the iceberg" (fig. 2.1). The real danger is below the waterline.

Clinicians usually address the visible symptoms of post-traumatic stress. These symptoms may include anger, sleeplessness, intrusiveness, hyperalertness, emotional numbing, dissociation, depression, and nightmares.

But there are symptoms that exist below the waterline. These symptoms might be grief, guilt, shame, anger toward God, alienation from him, and many forms of loss, such as loss of faith, loss of identity, and loss of meaning. These symptoms are spiritual in nature and require spiritual remedies. Some symptoms exist both above and below the waterline, requiring both clinical and spiritual intervention.

The below-the-waterline symptoms (fig. 2.1) represent significant spiritual symptoms of trauma that are not often addressed by mental health professionals. They frequently involve theological questions and existential concerns that are typically beyond the expertise of most clinicians. It is in these instances that pastoral caregivers are most helpful, because they are usually qualified to address the spiritual symptoms of trauma.

BELOW-THE-WATERLINE ISSUES OF TRAUMA

As I stated earlier, trauma usually involves loss. Much of this loss relates to the spiritual, to matters of faith, or to a violation of what is held sacred. These traumas may also lead to moral injury because they involve violations of what is right or betrayal of trust.[6] A sense of hopelessness, loss of trust, and lack of positive spontaneity also characterize spiritual trauma.[7]

Effects of wartime trauma have social and relational consequences. These consequences often involve the continuance of violence beyond the battlefield and the perpetration of abuse. Such consequences may lead to feelings of despair or hopelessness, and a deep sense of loneliness that may threaten the very stability of the soul.

The symptoms of spiritual trauma may manifest as conflicted belief systems and existential questioning. Deeply conflicted victims have lost their spiritual anchors and find themselves adrift, questioning basic assumptions about themselves, their values, and their beliefs.[8] Spirituality is at the center of existential questioning. These questions may include *Where did I come from and where am I headed? Who am I, how should I live, or what is my purpose? Or who or what am I connected to or how do I fit?*

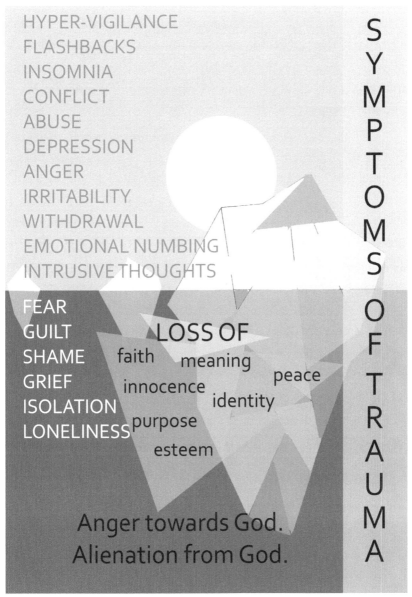

Figure 2.1: Symptoms of Trauma
Reprinted from Michael D. Bonura. Used by permission.

Existential questioning is a normal reaction to the experience of trauma. The search for meaning, for instance, generates great anxiety. If meaning is not found, the result can lead to total despair and confusion—an emotional, spiritual, or mental condition that is sometimes referred to as "the dark night of the soul."[9]

Trauma generates other spiritual questions about the nature of God, the suffering of the innocent, and the relationship of God to his creation. Trauma disrupts our ideas about ourselves. A traumatic event creates inner turmoil for victims, which some describe as disassociation between the inner self and the outer environment.[10] Coming to a resolution of the turmoil involves reintegrating the trauma so that the inner self is able to find meaning and purpose. When people make sense of their trauma, they also find peace.

Many servicemembers act as if they are invulnerable, but that sense of invulnerability is shattered when they become traumatized.[11]

Spiritual interventions must address the core issues of spiritual trauma. The use of biblical information about trauma to address these issues challenges traditional psychological interventions, which usually ignore the spiritual aspects of trauma. Addressing trauma in this way poses the possibility of new constructs for understanding trauma, and may mark the path for healing. Such new constructs radically alter the victims' understanding of their trauma and provide a way for finding healing and growth.[12]

THE SOLDIER AND SPIRITUAL TRAUMA

The spiritual effects of trauma are well documented among combat veterans. I've worked with warriors with extensive combat experience, and some indicated a loss of faith in God. Their combat experiences were intense and affected the way they viewed the world, themselves, or how they related to people close to them. Some of these members not only questioned God but also manifested other symptoms, such as loss of innocence or loss of meaning and purpose, often accompanied by severe guilt and grief reactions.[13]

Other servicemembers who were engaged in intensive combat told me how their experiences caused them to question their faith in God or their religious beliefs and practices. They appeared desperate and alone and often felt misunderstood. Their life stories were totally disrupted. They found it difficult to integrate their experiences with their beliefs and the way they wanted to live their lives. They were never at peace.

There is often a reduction in religious orientation among veterans diagnosed with PTSD. Though they may have once been active in church, those manifesting severe symptoms were now no longer active. They felt alone, powerless, and disenfranchised. In a study conducted by Wayne Chappelle, who served as an Air Force psychologist in Iraq, some warfighters withdrew from religious activities when they began to question their beliefs. This was especially the case after an attack and when a comrade was killed.[14] Veterans I've met and talked to found it difficult to reconnect to God or become spiritually active again after combat, despite strong belief in God or deep desire to practice their faith.

The extent to which spirituality exists in a veteran prior to combat affects the development of some trauma symptoms later. People who are more spiritually attuned, who are aware of themselves and God, and who possess an understanding of the world and the nature of evil are less likely to lose their faith as a consequence of trauma. Yet in instances of severe trauma, there is usually a decrease in faith or in spiritual growth regardless of spiritual maturity. There is also a greater likelihood of resentment toward God and prevalence of anger.

In cases of moderate trauma, servicemembers tend to express a positive outlook toward God despite continuing struggles with understanding their traumatic experiences. While growth is not often reported, most veterans I surveyed indicated a belief in the *potential* for spiritual growth and a reliance on spirituality or religion as significant factors leading to resilience during combat.[15]

Sometimes traumatized servicemembers seek new sources of meaning because of their doubts.[16] Former systems of beliefs prove inadequate for these members, and they cast about, looking for new answers, feeling alienated and abandoned by God.[17]

Some veterans perceive God's punishment in their traumatic symptoms and are unable to find forgiveness. Several studies report negative effects of religion among those with serious health problems.[18] Perceived punishment from God could imply blame or absence of forgiveness. Perceptions of an angry or unloving God foster fear, disillusionment, and distrust.

SPIRITUAL COPING AND TRAUMA

The experience of trauma may open the possibility for traumatized people to access their capacity for spiritual or religious coping. That is, they are capable of accessing spiritual resources that enable them to maintain their well-being despite adverse circumstances. Their values and beliefs help them withstand the negative effects of trauma so that they are able to bounce back quickly and resume normal functioning. This is certainly the teaching of Scripture. God uses adversity to develop character. He doesn't expect his children to avoid difficulties, affliction, or trauma. Rather, he uses them for his purposes, not only to develop character but also to increase faith and reliance upon him (Ps. 34:17–19; Isa. 41:10–13; Rom. 5:1–5; Jas. 1:2–4).

Some studies indicate that people find relief from the symptoms of their trauma through spiritual or religious coping.[19] In one study, people who used religious coping, nurtured by deep-seated convictions, were able to rise above their challenges.[20] In another study of 165 combat veterans with PTSD, which investigated the relationship between faith and quality of life, mental wellness was associated with positive spiritual coping.[21] The spiritual coping of these warriors was not always religious in nature or specifically Christian; nonetheless, spirituality or religion played an important role in enabling these warriors to sustain themselves during and after combat. Generally, people fare better when they have faith as a resource for coping.

Faith helps people accept what they cannot change and find peace despite the lack of definitive answers.[22] Religion is an important factor regardless of the context, whether it is trauma or some less severe circumstance. Religious content may even improve the effectiveness of psychotherapy. One study found that religious content improved the effectiveness of psychotherapy of the depressed, even when the therapist was not religious.[23]

Servicemembers who participate in religious activities experience a greater ability to cope with wartime adversity, a heightened sense of morale, and a positive sense of well-being. Chappelle observed an elevation of morale and a lowering of stress among warriors who actively participated in religious activities while deployed to OIF.[24] As a chaplain who conducted numerous worship services in combat, I noticed the calming and stabilizing effects religious services had upon Soldiers who attended worship or participated in Bible studies or prayer groups. Chappelle further noted an inclination in servicemembers to talk about their spiritual activities, which helped alleviate their suffering and pain.[25]

Spirituality—or religion, depending upon how one is inclined—contributes to resilience and the ability to cope with the negative effects of stress and trauma. But spirituality may also produce negative effects.

Spiritual Coping and Negative Effects

Some forms of spiritual or religious coping may contribute to negative outcomes, such as increased psychological or physical impairments. In one study, those who questioned God's love or perceived their situation as divine punishment or the work of the Devil experienced a significant increase in mortality.[26] They were found to be at a significant risk of dying over a two-year period.[27] Sometimes faith hinders coping or complicates recovery, especially in relation to anger, guilt, and shame.[28]

Spiritually motivated people may become conflicted and traumatized when they are compelled to violate their own sense of spirituality.[29] For example, a warfighter who kills a child to survive has much more trouble with the effects of his trauma than does a servicemember who kills an enemy combatant, because his actions violate his spiritual ethics. Similarly, servicemembers who have had to choose between saving a civilian or a comrade may suffer more from the effects of trauma.[30] These situations represent spiritual dilemmas that, if left unresolved, can lead to guilt.

Trauma, Benefits, and Spiritual Transformation

Trauma has the power to transform us and mold us into more compassionate and caring individuals.[31] In studies that examined the association between religious beliefs and trauma, the use of spirituality in therapeutic interventions proved beneficial for trauma victims.[32] Trauma exposes the depths of the soul and may initiate a process of spiritual inquiry and soul-searching. Trauma may serve as a "dark grace," leading one not to despair but to noble pursuits. For example, Saint Francis of Assisi used his wartime experience to propel him into a life of selfless service. Nelson Mandela turned his jail sentence into an opportunity to serve his country.[33]

Trauma brings to the forefront questions about the meaning of life, value in suffering, justice, forgiveness, and self-identity. These things become acute in the mind of the sufferer and must be answered. Deep issues that were hidden or on the periphery of consciousness are exposed by trauma. A traumatic event can break a person or create an opportunity to pursue a greater sense of meaning.[34]

Exploring spirituality and trauma raises the level of intervention to a transcendent plane that poses the possibility of new discoveries and new meanings.[35] Several studies noted the role of spirituality in the recovery of mental illness. Such recovery has meant new hope for the sufferers and a reclaiming of one's self, resulting in a renewed sense of meaning and purpose.[36] One study found that use of religious coping among the mentally ill contributed to their ongoing recovery. In a sample of 379 people, 81 percent reported the use of faith-based activities for coping, and 65 percent perceived the use of religious coping strategies to be effective.[37]

These studies point to the benefits of trauma when one is able to access religious or spiritual coping. While it is true that trauma sometimes produces a crisis of faith, it is also true that trauma sometimes opens the door to faith and combined with faith contributes to the sufferer's well-being and even transformation.

The role of chaplains, military and civilian, highlights the effective use of spiritual activities among those who are routinely stressed. I noted over my own career the effective use of spiritual activities among Soldiers under stress, including combat stress and at other times of great loss and suffering.

Some studies suggest symptoms like despair and discontentment may precipitate religious conversions.[38] At times of extreme difficulty, people are vulnerable and receptive to spiritual themes. They are often open to change and disposed to the prompting of the Holy Spirit. In a national survey conducted in 1988, 66 percent of the 1,481 respondents indicated death in the family often or sometimes strengthened their faith in God.[39] Many other studies, reports, and news stories highlight the power of faith in the lives of people who face severe trauma.

In a study of 154 Vietnam veterans that investigated the relationship of combat trauma to the presence of spirituality, certain beneficial aspects of spirituality (meaning and purpose, current worship attendance and prayer) correlated to long-term adjustment despite combat trauma. However, conflicts about faith and feelings of alienation from God correlated with more severe symptoms of PTSD.[40] In the same study, the researcher found frequent worship attendance was important because it indicated the presence of social support and a connectedness to God, which have been shown to support resiliency and contribute to healing.[41]

Spiritual well-being and the experience of trauma have a dynamic relationship. One study noted the causal relationship trauma has to well-being and to spirituality. The experience of trauma in a sample of respondents tended to decrease their well-being, which caused an increase in spirituality, which in turn restored well-being.[42]

So you can see from these studies, traumatic pain and suffering often have a positive impact on the development of one's spirituality and faith. However, pain and suffering could also have a negative impact on the development of one's spirituality and faith.

The Value of Spirituality and Spirituality-Based Treatment

The value of spirituality in the treatment of mental illness is gaining recognition among clinicians and other mental health professionals.[43] Though spirituality was long regarded as an unrelated concept, more and more mental health professionals are advocating an understanding of spirituality and its inclusion in treatment. However, most mental health professionals do not have the training to make spiritual interventions.

The healing of the person's spirit involves restoration to both life and community. Healing always involves transformation. Such transformation is not a return to conditions prior to the traumatic experience but an acquisition of new, adaptive ways of thinking and responding because of the trauma.[44]

The spiritual effects of trauma shatter one's sense of security and control. Spiritual intervention may account for that trauma and restore a sense of security and control. Many veterans report the importance and usefulness of spirituality in their lives. Veterans who have found Christ have seen their lives transformed. They've experienced God's love and forgiveness and are invigorated with hope and a sense of purpose they have not experienced before. Their relationships have been restored, and they've found meaning in service to others.[45]

Spirituality-based approaches to the treatment of PTSD are effective. Research shows that leveraging spirituality-based approaches produces results. In some cases, clinicians indicated they observed more results from spiritual interventions than from conventional behavioral health practices.[46]

In addressing religious coping as a useful process, Kenneth Pargament, internationally known for his work on religious beliefs and health, and his colleagues concluded the use of religious practices might be more responsive to the problem of human inadequacy than anything offered through conventional clinical interventions.[47] Veterans have overcome negative effects such as guilt and anger, and learned to let go of their bitterness through forgiveness.[48] These veterans found reconciliation with God and with others. They also gained courage and found hope.[49]

These observations are especially compelling given they are derived from research conducted by nonclerical caregivers. How much more effective might a clergyperson be who understands the spiritual nature of trauma and is able to apply spiritual remedies?

Some veterans suffer from alcoholism or drug abuse, and thus the shame that often goes with addiction. Many of these veterans report finding God and describe their experiences in terms of receiving God's grace and strength.[50] These reports should not be news to clergy. As pastors and chaplains, we have seen the power of God at work in the lives of those who are in our care. We know how the gospel changes lives. We know the power of forgiveness. We have witnessed people set free, redeemed from the bondage of guilt and shame.

GUIDELINES FOR THE IMPLEMENTATION OF SPIRITUAL COPING SKILLS

The following guidelines are useful for pastoral caregivers providing treatment for those suffering with the effects of trauma:

- Remain calm, composed, and in touch with your own feelings when interacting with anyone impacted by trauma.[51]

- Be aware of the profound theological questions post-trauma reflection produces.

- Be cognizant of your own beliefs and the limitations of those beliefs about suffering.

- Demonstrate an understanding of the levels of loss and the grieving process.

- Be aware of your professional limitations. While trauma is essentially a spiritual issue, it also presents many psychological complications, which are usually beyond the capability of the pastoral caregiver or Christian counselor. Consult with clinicians; do not hesitate to refer.

- Demonstrate sensitivity and respect for the veteran. Sensitivity and respect are especially critical because they help create a safe and secure environment that is essential for the treatment of PTSD. Never assume that you understand what a veteran has experienced.

- Use a client-centered approach that builds on trust and develops counselor-client rapport. Client-centered approaches focus on the needs and concerns of the client. The pastoral counselor who takes this approach begins where the client wants to begin and adjusts to the client's agenda as much as is reasonable and appropriate. This approach empowers the client and grants necessary control over treatment.

- Be sensitive to the spiritual perspectives of clients. When working with groups, the caregiver will encounter a wide range of spiritual perspectives. Some research suggests pastoral caregivers should avoid proselytizing the trauma victim and cautions practitioners to remain within the arena of their professional expertise. Other research indicates clients who voluntarily participate in spirituality-based programs are open to discussions about faith. Regardless, issues of faith should never be forced. It is always helpful for pastoral caregivers to consider the client's own sense of existence, beliefs, and practices and allow the client to open the door to more specific discussions about personal faith.[52]

Additional Guidelines and Observations

Pastoral caregivers should be prepared to respond to challenging theological questions. Spirituality-based treatment, especially involving orthodox Christian approaches, often includes theological questions about the source of evil, the purpose of suffering, and divine punishment. Christian counselors should exercise care when counseling someone who may be blaming God or who may be construing the terrible trauma they face, like the loss of a child, as intended somehow for their spiritual development.[53] Communicating or inferring these messages is not usually helpful and can be very damaging. We should not assume we know the mind of God. It is better to deal with the "what" and the "how" issues than the "why" concerns, at least in most cases.

Pastoral caregivers should avoid incorporating diverse spiritual teachings and methods into treatment. A practitioner may be tempted to experiment with different approaches, e.g., Native American or Eastern intervention techniques.[54] Some practitioners advocate an eclectic approach; for example, they draw from Greek mythology, Shamanism, and Buddhist rituals. I advise a more conservative approach, using practices and rituals familiar to the practitioner, and perhaps thereby avoiding retraumatizing the victim.

Pastoral caregivers should learn to assist the client in reconstructing spiritual beliefs in positive ways. How spiritual awareness develops depends upon the beliefs of the survivor. Undoubtedly, these beliefs will concern questions about the existence of God, the problem of evil, and the meaning and purpose of life.

Pastoral caregivers who are familiar with the concepts of spiritual direction may find these concepts useful in guiding a sufferer through the maze of suffering and in gaining a deeper understanding of the ways of God. Questions like *Where do you think God is in this?* or *What do you think God is saying to you through this experience?* may be helpful at appropriate times. We need to be sensitive to where our clients are and to what is happening to them. Good counselors know how to ask the right questions at the right time, and they are always sensitive to the needs of those who are in their care.

The Use of Spiritual Practices and Rituals

Prayer, meditation, and healing rituals are helpful in treating PTS.[55] In research I did with combat veterans, warriors most often identified prayer as the preferred spiritual coping activity.[56] Other productive forms of treatment include music therapy and guided imagery.[57] I have used thematic music and videos as well as pictures that depict therapeutic concepts during group sessions, and servicemembers have found them helpful.

Healing services have been developed and used successfully in promoting reconciliation.[58] Healing services are religious in nature and focus on confession, forgiveness, and reconciliation. They have been used to mark milestones in the treatment process or as celebratory events. They help servicemembers in the way they communalize their trauma. Communalization happens when the community acknowledges its role in sending servicemembers to war. It is the expression of the warrior's experience within the larger, supportive community.

In a feasibility study conducted by several researchers, the daily practice of repeating a sacred word or phrase throughout the day moderated symptoms of PTSD among a small sample of veterans. They found a reduction of psychological stress, a reduction in symptoms, and an increase in quality of life.

In research conducted by U.S. Army Chaplain Steve Hokana, spirituality-based writing produced positive states among veterans suffering with PTSD as opposed to writing that was not spiritually based.[59]

Spiritual healing can be found through confession. Confession is the admission of guilt. For many Christians, confession is an act of contrition that involves the sacrament of penance, of making amends for wrongs committed; it leads to reconciliation and absolution of sin. Veterans who are able to make things right with God and with offended parties are able to live with themselves. Some feel guilty for things they've done but without assigning the proportionate amount of guilt to others. They have carried a much too heavy and undeserved burden.

LIMITATIONS IN PASTORAL CARE

War involves killing, atrocities, and the loss of friends. Pastors who have not experienced war cannot imagine what it is like to be a combat veteran. They can listen, they can sympathize, but they will never completely understand.

Warriors do not expect civilians to understand. That's okay.

It is helpful for pastoral caregivers to recognize their limitations and not assume too much. Veterans want your respect, not your pity. Honor the veteran for his or her sacrifice; it will greatly contribute to your rapport with them. Don't assume every veteran needs to hear: "Thank you for your service." They may be ashamed of their service. Always affirm the veteran. Honor their sacrifice, including the sacrifices made by their families.

A pastor or chaplain represents God. This may be an obstacle for the veteran who has blamed God for their trauma. Patience, compassion, and humility lead to the development of a bond of trust between the pastoral caregiver and servicemember. Eventually, theological questions will surface, and it is important for the pastoral caregiver to provide honest and sensitive responses.

The pastoral counselor serves as a spiritual guide, encouraging the veteran to accept responsibility for wartime actions and leading the warrior in confession and reconciliation with God. This is an enormous task, requiring spiritual companionship and commitment.[60]

The Role of the Church in the Communalization of Trauma

The prevalence of PTS in the community demands a response from the church. The church can play an effective role in addressing PTS among its members and as an outreach to the community, especially in the role of communalizing trauma.

Communalization of trauma is the victim's expression of trauma, its effects, and its personal impact within a larger and supportive community, such as a church. The church is a redemptive community in which servicemembers suffering from PTS find compassion, forgiveness, love, and reconciliation. As a faith community, the church offers numerous opportunities for victims to exchange their loneliness and isolation for restoration and reconnection.[61]

As a context for healing, the redemptive community provides soil for the cultivation of one's wholeness. Members relate to one another without fear or recrimination. The church provides a context for the expression of unconditional love and a network of support for the pastor and the survivor.

Within the church, God has placed people who minister with their gifts, offering the means to restoration and connectedness, and bridging the gap that exists between loneliness and belonging.[62] The church is a healing community, a community where people are loved and accepted, and a place where each person is affirmed and empowered.

Healing begins in the context of communalization, when survivors treat survivors, and the larger community gives its support. It occurs in the context of a community of trust which fosters total, unconditional regard. Veterans feel comfortable telling their stories in a community of like-minded veterans within a larger, supportive community of civilians who do not pretend to understand but who truly care.

It is the larger community that must take responsibility for sending servicemembers to war. The community has an obligation to the veteran because we are in this together. The community has a responsibility to support veterans upon their return from combat and help in the process of their healing. The church within the larger community can certainly lead the way.

Notes

1. A. Gurney and S. Rogers, "Object-Relations and Spirituality: Revisiting a Clinical Dialogue," *Journal of Clinical Psychology* 63, no. 10 (2007): 964.
2. Ibid.
3. Ronald Rolheiser, *The Holy Longing* (New York: Doubleday, 1999); T. Plante, "What Do the Spiritual and Religious Traditions Offer the Practicing Psychologist?" *Pastoral Psychology* 56 (2008): 429–444; Kent Drescher, "Treatment of Moral and Spiritual Injuries Associated with PTSD" (seminar conducted at the Naval Medical Center, Portsmouth, VA, September 12, 2013).
4. Larry Decker, "Including Spirituality," National Center for PTSD Clinical Quarterly 5, no. 1 (1995): 1; Plante, "What Do," 430; Kenneth Pargament, *The Psychology of Religion and Coping: Theory, Research, Practice* (New York: Guilford Press, 1997), 36; Pargament et al., "The Sacred."
5. Grant, "Spirituality and Trauma," 1; Mahoney et al., "Broken Vows."
6. Shay, *Achilles in Vietnam*.
7. Daléne Fuller-Rogers, *Pastoral Care* for Post-traumatic Stress Disorder (New York: Haworth Pastoral Press, 2002); N. Duncan Sinclair, *Horrific Traumata: A Pastoral Response to the Post-traumatic Stress Disorder* (New York: Haworth Pastoral Press, 1993); Brené Brown, "Shame Resilience Theory: A Grounded Theory on Women and Shame," *Families in Society* 87, no. 1, vol. 4 (2006): 3–52; Kent Drescher and David Foy, "Spirituality and Trauma Treatment: Suggestions for Including Spirituality as a Coping Resource," *National Center for PTSD Clinical Quarterly* 5, no. 1 (1995): 4–5.
8. Sherry A. Falsetti, Patricia A. Resick, and Joanne L. Davis, "Changes in Religious Beliefs Following Trauma," *Journal of Traumatic Stress* 16, no. 4 (2003): 392.
9. Daryl S. Paulson, "The Hard Issues of Life," *Pastoral Psychology* 49, no. 5 (2001): 385–394. This phrase is attributed to St. John of the Cross (1542–1591), who was a Spanish mystic and Catholic priest, and used the phrase to describe his lack of Christian joy. The "dark night" is a time of spiritual dryness, spiritual shadows, and spiritual struggle; it is time when God appears withdrawn from the individual.
10. Decker, "Including Spirituality."
11. Ibid.
12. Raymond Finch, "Trauma and Forgiveness: A Spiritual Inquiry," Journal of Spirituality in Mental Health 9, no. 2 (2006): 27–41.
13. For an extensive discussion of these reactions, see Herman, *Trauma and Recovery*; Pargament et al., "The Sacred"; Margaret Nelson-Pechota, "Spirituality and PTSD in Vietnam Combat Veterans," *National Conference of Vietnam Veteran Ministers*, accessed December 1, 2015, http://www.vietnamveteranministers.org/spirituality_intro.htm.
14. Wayne Chappelle, "An Air Force Psychologist's Collaboration With Clergy: Lessons Learned on the Battlefield of Iraq," *Journal of Psychology and Christianity* 25, no. 3 (2006): 205–215.

15. Dean Bonura, "A Biblical Approach to the Problem of PTSD," (DMin dissertation, Gordon-Conwell Theological Seminary, 2009).

16. Pargament et al., "The Sacred"; Nelson-Pechota, "Spirituality and PTSD."

17. Nelson-Pechota, "Spirituality and PTSD."

18. See Pargament et al., "The Sacred" for the studies they cite.

19. Weaver et al., "A Systematic Review."

20. As cited in M. Eberly, "Resiliency: Bouncing Back From Adversity," *Christian Counseling Today* 14, no. 4 (2006): 36–39; see also S. Joseph and P. A. Linley, "Psychological Assessment of Growth Following Adversity: A Review" in *Trauma, Recovery, and Growth*, eds. Stephen Joseph and P. Alex Linley (Hoboken, NJ: Wiley, 2008), 21–36; Evelyn F. Bussema and Kenneth E. Bussema, "Gilead Revisited: Faith and Recovery," *Psychiatric Rehabilitation Journal* 30, no. 4 (2007): 301–305.

21. T. Rouss, "Religiousness/Spirituality and Quality of Life in Combat Veterans with Posttraumatic Stress Disorder," (PhD dissertation, Pepperdine University, 2006); Bussema and Bussema, "Gilead Revisited."

22. Schiraldi, *The Post-Traumatic Stress Disorder Source Book: A Guide to Healing, Recovery, and Growth*.

23. Ibid.

24. Chappelle, "An Air Force Psychologist's."

25. Ibid.

26. As cited in Pargament et al., "The Sacred."

27. Ibid., 677.

28. Bussema and Bussema, "Gilead Revisited," 386.

29. Matsakis, *Post-traumatic*.

30. Ibid.

31. Grant, "Spirituality and Trauma," 1.

32. Falsetti et al., "Changes in Religious Beliefs," 391–398. See also Weaver et al., "A Systematic Review."

33. Richard Scheinin, "Trauma May Open a Door to Spirituality," *The Gazette* (1998–99), accessed December 10, 2015, http://www.ptsdsupport.net/gazette.html.

34. Ibid.

35. Finch, "Trauma and Forgiveness."

36. Ibid.

37. Bussema and Bussema, "Gilead Revisited." See also Bonura, "A Biblical Approach," who observed from a study of 30 OIF/OEF veterans, that most indicated they felt indebted to God in some way for preserving their lives or acknowledged that a Transcendent Being was with them in combat. Soldiers who were reporting PTSD symptoms did not blame God or express unbelief but frequently admitted they struggled with their faith, or conversely that their faith in God was the only anchor they had as they tried to live with their PTSD. Many Soldiers reported some reliance on spirituality as a coping tool during combat. Many indicated prayer, attendance at worship services, and religious beliefs helped them cope.

38.   As cited in James E. Kennedy, Robert C. Davis, and Bruce G. Taylor, "Changes in Spirituality and Well-being Among Victims of Sexual Assault," *Journal for the Scientific Study of Religion* 37, no. 2 (1998): 322–328.

39.   Ibid.

40.   Nelson-Pechota, "Spirituality and PTSD."

41.   Ibid.

42.   Kennedy et al., "Changes in Spirituality," 326.

43.   Weaver et al., "A Systematic Review."

44.   Sinclair, *Horrific Traumata*; C. Adsit, *The Combat Trauma Healing Manual* (Newport News, VA: Military Ministry Press, 2007); Margaret Hill, Harriet Hill, Richard Baggé, and Pat Miersma, *Healing the Wounds of Trauma: How the Church Can Help* (Nairobi: Paulines Publications Africa, 2004).

45.   Dewey, *War and Redemption*.

46.   Ibid.

47.   Pargament et al., "The Sacred."

48.   Dewey, *War and Redemption*.

49.   Ibid.

50.   Ibid.

51.   Fuller-Rogers, *Pastoral Care*; Drescher and Foy, "Spirituality and Trauma Treatment."

52.   Fuller-Rogers, *Pastoral Care*.

53.   Ibid.

54.   Tick, *War and the Soul*.

55.   Fuller-Rogers, *Pastoral Care*.

56.   Bonura, "A Biblical Approach."

57.   Philip G. Salois, "Spiritual Healing and PTSD," National Center for PTSD Clinical Quarterly 5, no. 1 (1995): 12; Fuller-Rogers, *Pastoral Care*.

58.   Salois, "Spiritual Healing and PTSD."

59.   Steve Hokana, "The Body of Christ in the Presence of Their Pain," *Caring Connections: An Inter-Lutheran Journal for Practitioners and Teachers of Pastoral Care and Counseling* 4, no. 3 (2007): 13–16.

60.   Fuller-Rogers, *Pastoral Care*.

61.   Ibid.

62.   Ibid.

Chapter 3

The Problem of Grief

We shake our heads, but whether it be the lost years that
remain there, or the comrades who lie there, or all the misery
that this earth covers—there is a grief in our bones, enough to
make us howl aloud.

—Erich M. Remarque, *The Road Back*

A VETERAN was deeply disturbed by the loss of his friends in a war. We met at his place of employment, where he shared some of his most painful memories from that war. He was close to his friends, and when their situation became uncertain, he was concerned for their safety. It was not until many months later that he finally learned that they had been killed in action. This loss was hard for him to bear. He felt that if he had only been there when they were killed, things might have turned out differently. He might have been able to prevent their deaths. He felt responsible in some ways for their deaths, and this contributed to his feelings of guilt. This loss was only compounded by additional horrible losses that he later experienced in combat.

Grief doesn't get any easier for leaders. Over a sixteen-month tour in Afghanistan, an infantry battalion lost twenty Soldiers and 120 wounded. One senior leader commented:

Some of my Soldiers who were killed were close to me ... There are times when I dream about the Soldiers I put in bags and I see all of their faces. One trigger is when I walk into the battalion headquarters and see the memorial display. You think about what happened to them. I have a picture of them in my mind, what they looked like after they were killed. I think everyone has a sense of grief about the comrades they lose.[1]

Grief is devastating for veterans. Eugene Sledge, who served as a Marine in the Pacific during World War II, suffered with grief his whole life after the war. He participated in some of the most savage fighting on the islands of Peleliu and Okinawa, and upon hearing of the death of his commanding officer, he recorded these words in his diary:

We felt forlorn and lost. It was the worse grief I endured during the entire war. The intervening years have not lessened it any.... The loss of many close friends grieved me deeply on Peleliu and Okinawa. But to all of us the loss of our company commander at Peleliu was like losing a parent we depended upon for security— not our physical security, because we knew that was a commodity beyond our reach in combat, but our mental security.[2]

Grief is a significant issue for many veterans returning from combat. While grief is universally experienced, it manifests differently in combat veterans and warrants our examination.[3]

Grief encompasses an array of emotional, behavioral, cognitive, and physiological components: such as insomnia, preoccupation with the dead, loss of appetite, and social withdrawal. But what does grief mean?

DEFINING GRIEF

The problem with grief may stem from injustices, anger, or brutalities. It typically results from a loss, such as a death, and it leads to intense forms of mental, emotional, and spiritual suffering.[4] Grief involves inner personal turmoil and inevitably means some kind of accommodation to change. John James and Russell Friedman characterize grief in *The Grief Recovery Handbook* as conflicted feelings that result from a change in behavior or as an end to a familiar pattern of behavior.[5] Below, we'll consider three types of grief that are particularly associated with veterans who suffer with PTS.

Complicated Grief

Complicated grief stems from trauma and is attended by feelings of sadness, emotional pain, sleeplessness, and inner turmoil that are typical of grief. It includes symptoms of ongoing intrusiveness, numbness, and feelings of helplessness.[6] This grief manifests in a host of existential issues often faced by the combatant, such as personal vulnerability, survivor's guilt, and loss of meaning. These additional factors complicate grief and make it more difficult to manage.

Servicemembers suffering in this way feel vulnerable in combat, especially when they realize that the death of a fellow servicemember could easily have been their own deaths. It creates a personal crisis. I often thought about warriors who were killed in the very places and on the very roads I traveled. It preyed on my mind, and I wondered if I would be next to die. I not only grieved over the loss of my Soldiers but also grieved my own possible demise.

Chronic Grief

Many veterans report problems with longstanding, unresolved grief. They never fully get over their losses. The losses always nag at their souls. While it is not necessary to forget one's loss, chronic grief becomes a problem when it's a lengthy preoccupation, inhibiting quality of life and contributing to occupational and social dysfunction.

Disenfranchised Grief

A third type is disenfranchised grief, which manifests as complicated grief in servicemembers.[7] It's often misunderstood and not shared with civilians. Servicemembers feel left out, unable to share their pain because most civilians don't understand how grief affects veterans. Therefore, this grief is never publicly mourned, acknowledged, or supported. It is for these reasons our veterans continue to suffer alone and without any relief.

Most veterans are not inclined to share their most horrible experiences and deepest losses. When these losses are not acknowledged, they are often dismissed by the uninformed. The loss of any warfighter is a loss to all servicemembers. Even today, I grieve the loss of any warrior whether I knew him or not. The pain swells up inside and I mourn their loss and grieve for their family. The fraternity of warriors is bound by deep commitments to one another. This is disenfranchised grief: it is a grief society does not understand or share.

NONCOMBATANT LOSSES

Colonel Charles Hoge, retired, who served on a mental health advisory team in Iraq, reported that 14–28 percent of the Soldiers he surveyed said they were directly responsible for killing a noncom-batant in Iraq or Afghanistan.[8] The loss of noncombatants creates a moral dissonance that tears at the warrior's soul. Even in cases where legitimate targets have been killed, the experience of killing has an unsettling effect on most warriors. Sometimes the effect manifests as self-doubt, sometimes as spiritual questioning. That's because it's not normal for a human being to take another human life. Killing has awful consequences.[9]

In the instances when civilians are killed, whether by design or by accident, no logical argument can compel sufferers to feel differ-ently about their actions. While on duty in Iraq in 2003, I counseled a Soldier who had mistakenly killed a civilian. A car approached his checkpoint and failed to heed his warnings. He engaged the vehi-cle with his weapon and stopped the vehicle. The driver was dead and apparently had had no malicious intent. Unfortunately, the Soldier could not know that. He was forced to open fire to stop the vehicle, which easily could have been laden with explosives. His actions did not violate military directives for the use of force, also known as the rules of engagement (ROE), but he was nevertheless left deeply disturbed by the tragic event. He blamed himself alone for the civilian's death.

Such lamentable events are traumatic and lead to all forms of grief, including guilt and shame. Understanding their powerful effects on servicemembers will make the pastoral caregiver more prepared to deal with them when they arise in treatment.

MANAGING GRIEF IN COMBAT
Dealing with grief during combat operations presents challenges and has consequences. Veterans report they must protect them-selves from grieving too deeply at the risk of losing their combat

edge.[10] The mission dictates operational tempo (the pace and frequency of military operations), and warriors are afforded limited opportunities to grieve the deaths of comrades. The fallen are always mourned, and memorials are conducted quickly and solemnly to honor the fallen and provide space for the living to grieve. Servicemembers build protective shields to insulate themselves from the emotional effects of their losses. One consequence is emotional numbing that remains with the servicemember after returning from the war.[11] Numbing often affects social relationships, particularly marital and family intimacy, and may lead to depression later on.

Allowing for the expression of grief in a combat environment, despite the intention to provide closure, is not sufficient to address the grieving process and the lingering problem of grief. More must be done. Pastoral caregivers should be cognizant of the presence of unresolved grief among veterans returning from combat, and make an effort to address this need. The church is an excellent place for our veterans to find the support they need to resolve their grief.

THE BIBLICAL CONCEPT OF GRIEF

The Scriptures acknowledge the emotions of grief, anger, loss, and sadness. Grieving is appropriate and normal. Jacob grieved the loss of Joseph (Gen. 37:34–35). Job grieved his losses: his children, his prestige, his wealth, and his health. David grieved several losses: the loss of Saul and Jonathan (2 Sam. 1), the loss of Abner, his military commander (2 Sam. 3:31–39), and the loss of Absalom, his son (2 Sam. 18:31–19:1). Naomi suffered from multiple losses: her husband and her two sons (Ruth 1). Jesus grieved the loss of Lazarus (John 11:35), and he lamented the faithlessness of Jerusalem (Matt. 23:37–39). Grief is a universal emotion.

The Scriptures teach that God is the great Comforter of the soul, and those who grieve may not only experience God's comfort themselves but help others experience the same comfort by their own experience with loss (2 Cor. 1). Practitioners help the grieving by pointing them to the "God of all comfort" and allowing for the process of grief (2 Cor. 1:3; 1 Thess. 4:13).

The Bible encourages believers to rest in the hope of eternal life (John 6:37–40; John 10:28; 1 John 3:2–3; 1 John 5:11–12; 1 Thess. 4:13–18; 1 Pet. 1:3–7), and to take courage in God despite temporal suffering and loss (Heb. 10:32–39; Job 19:25–26). Death is not the end; Christ's victory over death provides the evidence for life beyond this world (1 Cor. 15). Indeed, Paul's conclusions about death in 1 Corinthians 15 hinge on the resurrection of Christ: "And if Christ has not been raised, your faith is futile and you are still in your sins ... But in fact Christ has been raised from the dead, the first fruits of those who have fallen asleep" (v. 17–18). Jesus' resurrection guarantees the resurrection of all believers in Christ.

Jesus echoes this sentiment in his statement to Martha upon the death of Lazarus: "I am the resurrection and the life. Whoever believes in me, though he die, yet shall he live, and everyone who lives and believes in me shall never die" (John 11:25–26). First-century Christians at Thessalonica were reminded that their losses attended by grief were not without hope (1 Thess. 4:13). John, writing in the book of Revelation, concluded there is coming a day when God "will wipe away every tear ... and death shall be no more, neither shall there be mourning nor crying nor pain anymore" (Rev. 21:4).

Death for a Christian is not the end nor a loss but rather an eternal gain (Phil. 1:21–24). The apostle Paul understood death as an appointed departure and a completion of a mission (2 Tim. 4:6–8). The psalmist, David, penned the beautiful poetry of the

Shepherd's Psalm, which promises God's presence in the "valley of the shadow of death" (Ps. 23:4; see also Ps. 16). God will never leave or abandon his children (Heb. 13:5–6). He promises a place for them after death (John 14:1–3), bidding them to take comfort and courage from his promise of the resurrection (John 11:25–26). The death of a child of God is precious in the sight of God (Ps. 116:15). All of these facts temper the grieving process for believers and enable recovery.

THE STORY OF NEHEMIAH (NEH. 1:1–2:8)

Nehemiah's name means "the Comfort of Yahweh" or "God has comforted." His response to loss is instructive and shows us how God brings his children through the grieving process to a place of recovery, reconciliation, and renewal.

Nehemiah deeply grieved the losses experienced by the Jewish remnant that had survived the exile in Jerusalem. He was troubled by the shame the remnant was experiencing because the wall of Jerusalem was in shambles and its gates had been destroyed (Neh. 1:2–3). Nehemiah, who would later lead a contingent of men to Jerusalem to rebuild the walls and defend the city, expressed his grief for days through weeping, fasting, and praying (Neh. 1:4).

Turning to God in prayer in the midst of grief, Nehemiah gained some perspective on his situation. Despite his ongoing sadness, he took the opportunity to express his concerns to the king (Neh. 2:2). This act of faith led to the granting of his petition and eventual intervention in Jerusalem, which culminated in a great achievement. Throughout this process, Nehemiah sensed God's presence (Neh. 2:8). The road ahead for Nehemiah was not particularly easy, but he remained optimistic. God honored him for his faith, comforted him in his grief, and blessed his efforts.

Psalm 30 reminds us that God remains with us in our grief and pain. He hears our prayers and turns our "mourning into dancing," removing our sackcloth and clothing us "with gladness" (Ps. 30:11).

The words of Horatio Spafford (1828–88), who lost all four of his daughters in a disaster at sea, are fitting here:

> *When peace like a river attendeth my way,*
> *When sorrows like sea-billows roll;*
> *Whatever my lot, Thou hast taught me to say,*
> *It is well with my soul.*
> *Tho' Satan should buffet, tho' trials should come;*
> *Let this blest assurance control;*
> *That Christ hath regarded my helpless estate*
> *And hath shed His own blood for my soul.*
> *And, Lord, haste the day when my faith shall be sight,*
> *The clouds be rolled back as a scroll,*
> *The trump shall resound, and the Lord shall descend;*
> *"Even so" it is well with my soul.*

THE DIMENSIONS OF THE GRIEVING PROCESS

The grieving process has often been explained in terms of stages or dimensions.[12] Erich Lendemann, formerly chief of psychiatry at Massachusetts General Hospital in Boston and known for his extensive work on grief, was one of the first to describe grief in terms of stages. He based his work on interviews he conducted in 1942 with survivors of Boston's Coconut Grove fire.[13]

Elizabeth Kübler-Ross, in discussing the process of dying, identified five stages of grief: 1) denial, 2) anger, 3) bargaining, 4) depression, and 5) acceptance. Her five-stage description is well known and has become the formula for understanding grief. Others have identified additional stages of grief. Granger Westberg, author of the bestselling book *Good Grief*, identifies ten stages, ranging from initial shock through various emotional and physical expressions to feelings of hope and acceptance.[14]

Regardless of how we view grief, researchers generally agree that stages of grief do not necessarily reflect how every person experiences grief. Grief is unique to each person, and while many will experience the emotions identified in the various stages of grief, grief is not the same for everyone. Neither does every person necessarily go through all of the stages or in any particular order. Dr. Alan Wolfelt, in *Companioning the Bereaved: A Soulful Guide for Caregivers*, thinks the range of grieving emotions expressed in various stages tends to depict a movement from disorganization to reorganization, or a movement from shock to a place of acceptance, where new relationships are established.[15]

John James and Russell Friedman, in *The Grief Recovery Handbook*, argue there aren't any stages of grief at all, only a range of emotions that people experience. Anger is often identified as a stage of grief. But anger is not always associated with grief. Many deaths or other losses involve no anger at all. It is inappropriate to assume anger is a stage everyone goes through.[16]

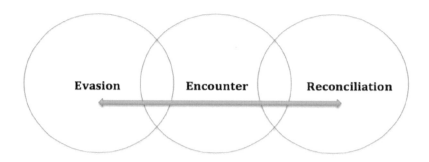

Figure 3.1: Wolfelt's Grieving Process

Alan Wolfelt, instead of stages, prefers to describe the journey of grief in terms of three broad dimensions: "evasion, encounter, and reconciliation."[17] His three dimensions of grief provide a useful framework for understanding how grief works.

EVASION

Most people evade grief through shock, denial, emotional numbing, or disbelief. Anticipated loss tends to diminish the effects of these evading emotions, while unanticipated grief can produce the full range of evasive emotions. The onset of sudden grief may produce comments like *I felt like I was in a dream* or *I can't believe this is happening to me*. How and when a person moves from this dimension depends upon the individual.

At some point, the grief journey brings a person to a realization of the loss. This realization usually comes in the first six weeks following a death. However, events such as an anniversary or other special occasion can trigger an emotional grief cycle all over again.

Grief is more like a spectrum of emotions. A person travels back and forth on a continuum, re-experiencing the same emotions over and over again as they struggle to accept the meaning and reality of the loss.[18]

ENCOUNTER

During the encounter phase, servicemembers may experience a wide range of emotions from outbursts of anger and brooding hostility to general anxiety, panic, or fear. The loss of a comrade creates a sense of insecurity for the grieving person. Feelings of insecurity may evolve into anxiety or panic. Many warfighters express deep sadness. This pervasive sadness and anxiety may produce feelings of being abnormal or overwhelmed, or cause an inability to concentrate sufficiently to complete simple tasks. Along with this, a warfighter may experience physiological changes such as headaches, heart palpitations, shortness of breath, or insomnia.

Dynamic Emotions and Other Expressions of Grief

Anger, hostility, and rage or acts of hatred, revenge, and atrocity are often connected to grief in the combat veteran—but not always. Deprivation, exposure to violence, perceived injustice, and loss of meaning or control represent other causes for the expression of these dynamic emotions or actions. Keep in mind that while these are associated with PTS, they are not always directly related to the grieving process.[19] Dynamic emotions are connected to other issues, such as guilt and shame.

Anger

During the grieving process, a person's anger may become evident. Anger or irritability is always associated with PTS, and it's especially an issue for veterans who are suffering with grief. Anger has a lot to do with the experience of prolonged stress that has never been diffused. In research conducted among thirty veterans within two years after returning from combat, nearly half reported issues with anger, irritability, or aggressive behavior. In a survey of 165 Iraq war veterans, there were seventy-five reports of angry, irritable, or aggressive behavior. Anger is a huge problem.[20]

Anger usually accompanies other emotions, such as depression and guilt. There are various reasons for anger. They include anger over the traumatic event itself, the effects of the trauma upon the person or those associated with the person, and all forms of loss.[21] Anger in a grieving person may indicate a range of primary emotions from helplessness and fear to frustration.[22] The expression of these emotions can be helpful because they are needed to bring the person to a place of reconciliation.[23]

A very common expression of anger is anger directed at God or his representative. It is not necessary to judge someone's anger. It can be quite understandable. Caregivers can best assist the grieving person by allowing them room for their anger.[24]

Another common expression of anger is anger directed inwardly. Self-directed anger is associated with survivor's guilt.[25] Anger may manifest in the veteran in the form of guilt, depression, or diminished self-worth.[26] Probing below the surface of these manifestations will likely reveal some perceived or real failure.

The problem of anger in the grieving person is sometimes complicated by feelings of resentment, self-blame, blame toward others, hatred, or jealousy.[27] Sometimes the mourner has rage, and this leads to other problems if not managed appropriately.[28] The ongoing problem of domestic violence in the military illustrates, in part, some detrimental and dangerous results of mismanaged rage. But not all instances of domestic violence should be attributed to service-members with PTS or expressions of grief.

Anger can trigger intrusive thoughts and feelings. The sight of comrades being hit by enemy fire can cause a warrior to feel sickened, angry, and frustrated. Enemy fire can come suddenly out of nowhere, and the warrior may never even see the enemy. When my convoy was attacked in Iraq and we sustained a casualty, we wanted to fight back, but the enemy was nowhere to be found. It makes you really angry.

Problems with anger persist long after combat. One of my Soldiers went through a period of anger after he returned from the war. One day he became very angry and was ready to give up. His command referred him to behavioral health.

Sometimes it is not so much the combat trauma that brings out post-trauma anger as it is dysfunctional units and failed leadership. A Soldier I once counseled was mostly frustrated and angry over how his unit treated him. Despite his efforts to find resolution, he was unsuccessful and left combat embittered, cynical, and angry.

The goal of treatment for anger is to get beyond the acknowledged and legitimate anger. It requires spiritual interventions that address the need for forgiveness from others, forgiveness from God, or forgiveness of one's self. It is helpful for those who struggle with anger to know that God not only forgives, he understands.[29]

Hostility and Rage

Hostility or rage toward the enemy is a common emotional response among veterans and often associated with PTS. An OIF veteran told me about the hostility he felt toward the enemy. He had seen numerous wounded Americans, and it had deeply affected him. He felt the enemy was heartless and operated without compassion or regard for women and children. He thought they were cowards, lacking any sense of right and wrong. For that, he hated them and held them in utter disdain.

J. Glenn Gray, who served in combat during World War II, describes in his excellent book, *The Warriors: Reflections of Men in Battle*, an extreme form of rage that fuels revenge in warfighters: "[It is a] fury that makes them capable of anything. Blinded by the rage to destroy and supremely careless of consequences, they storm against the enemy until they are either [sic] victorious, dead, or utterly exhausted. It is as if they are seized by a demon and are no longer in control of themselves."[30]

This kind of rage is like a "red fog." The account of Ernst Juenger from World War I, cited by Gray, describes it graphically: "The great moment had come. The curtain of fire lifted from the front trenches.

We stood up. With mixture of feelings, evoked by bloodthirstiness, rage, and intoxication, we moved in step … toward the enemy lines … I was boiling with mad rage, which had taken hold of me … Rage pressed bitter tears from my eyes. The monstrous desire for annihilation, which hovered over the battlefield, thickened the brains of the men and submerged them in a red fog."[31]

Leaders monitor feelings of hatred, acts of rage, and disrespect for the enemy. In combat, units and individual warriors may look for revenge as an "eye for an eye." Rage is like a beast. It can raise its ugly head anytime. "Leadership controls the beast," according to one leader. Leaders enforce the ROE and ensure their servicemembers understand those rules before each combat patrol. They exist to protect the lives of servicemembers.

Some warriors may disrespect their opponent. While we do not have to like the enemy, we must respect them—that is, respect their military capabilities as one might respect the lethality of a rattlesnake. A senior leader commented: "I highly respect the enemy. My grandfather told me after I was trashing a football team we had just beaten to knock it off. I don't believe the enemy is fighting for the right cause. He believes in his cause and wants to fight me. I don't think they show the same care or respect for us. He's crafty and innovative, and he knows how to fight; but I have trouble with the way he treats prisoners, and the way the enemy desecrate remains."[32]

Hatred, Revenge, and Atrocities

War and its consequences not only incite anger, rage, or hostility but also uncontrolled hatred, acts of revenge, and atrocity toward the enemy. In some cases, servicemembers go berserk over the loss of comrades and commit atrocities or acts of revenge because they are seeking payback. The history of war is replete with lamentable acts perpetrated by all sides, aggressor and defender. Numerous accounts speak of grief over losses that led to murderous brutality that fueled hatred for the enemy and contributed to savage fighting and acts of revenge.

People are capable of enormous evil and cruelty. On Peleliu, Eugene Sledge was horrified to watch a fellow Marine extract with his service issue knife the gold teeth from a disabled Japanese soldier. After several unsuccessful attempts, the Marine cut the man's cheeks from ear to ear to extract the teeth.[33]

During my combat tour in Iraq, an officer in my brigade shot to death an unarmed, wounded prisoner. In another incident, the enemy captured, tortured, and burned four military contractors and hanged the remains of two of them from a bridge in Fallujah. Isis repeatedly brutalizes the innocent, beheading civilians and combatants alike without remorse.

Atrocities are one of the most difficult factors to overcome in the treatment of PTSD.[34] The memory of such actions is difficult to suppress and leads to a negative cycle of self-blame.[35] Servicemembers manifesting these symptoms encounter difficulty in seeking or accepting forgiveness. In some instances, warriors numb themselves, displaying no emotion and accepting no blame.

In a study of atrocities involving Vietnam veterans, Sarah A. Haley reported in the *Archives of General Psychiatry* that atrocities are "illegitimate" war activities that carry justifiable moral consequences.[36] Given there exists a moral dimension to any atrocity, treatment must be tailored differently from the treatment of those suffering from stress as a result of legitimate war activities. Haley cautions clinicians to exercise care due to differences that exist between existential issues and interpersonal or social dysfunction issues. Existential issues, Haley argues, spill over into a transcendent realm where resolution requires an examination that is based on moral judgments. It is an area encumbered by ambiguities and potential pitfalls.

Hence, it is incumbent on pastoral caregivers, who are best equipped to address existential questions, to understand the nature of atrocities, hatred for the enemy, and acts of revenge. They occur in every war, and warfighters return bearing the marks of these actions on their hearts and souls.

Confusion and Disorganization

As the reality of loss sets in, confusion or disorganization develops in the mourner. The grieving individual is often unable to complete tasks or projects and tends to become agitated, impatient, and restless.[37] He or she may feel disoriented. Some mourners become preoccupied with the deceased, searching or yearning for them, or become distracted by their memories. Sometimes hallucinations occur or people imagine the deceased person is actually with them. Some suffer from sleeplessness and lack of appetite. The grieving person may experience frequent dreams about the person they've lost.[38]

Loss, Emptiness, and Sadness

Grieving individuals often encounter feelings of loss, emptiness, and sadness. A full sense of loss evolves over time. Feelings of loss are often associated with a sense of isolation and loneliness. These various feelings of loss and sadness may lead to clinical depression.

Feelings of deprivation and impoverishment accompany sadness and emptiness. Such feelings are common among grieving persons, indicating the desire for the comfort and company of the deceased. Often there is a sense of relief expressed by the grieving person. For a servicemember, this may be due to the realization of being spared from death because someone else died. Crying and expressing thoughts and feelings about the loss also produce a sense of relief.

Depression

Depression is often associated with the onset of PTS.[39] Depression is a predictable and normal response. It manifests in various forms.

It's important to distinguish between depressive grief and clinical depression. Depressive grief is temporary and responsive to support. But clinical depression is usually long lasting and less responsive to support. Clinicians will often diagnose severe depression as clinical depression, which interferes with normal functioning. Symptoms of this kind of depression may include problems with concentration, insomnia, changes in eating habits, sense of loss, fatigue, or restlessness.[40]

Clinically depressive persons resist support, repress anger, express a sense of "doom and gloom," project hopelessness, and present a deep loss of self-esteem.[41] Pastoral caregivers should usually defer to mental health professionals when dealing with symptoms that present as clinical depression.

RECONCILIATION

Reconciliation represents the third and final dimension of the grieving process according to Wolfelt. Movement to the place of reconciliation is indicated when the grieving person begins to acknowledge the permanence of the loss. The reality of the loss is accepted, the pain has been experienced and acknowledged, and the person adjusts to an environment that no longer includes the person who has been lost. The grief-stricken person arrives at a new normalcy.[42] At this point a person is able to integrate the changes produced by the loss and express a new sense of meaning and purpose. This is evident by a renewed confidence, reinvested energy, and a new outlook on life.[43]

Reconciliation is an ongoing process in which there are new realizations about the loss and acceptance of the grief experience. A person comes to reconciliation with the realization that the loss can never be replaced. It involves accepting the consequences and effects of the loss. It is acceptance of the cold reality of finality. From this point, the grieving person can choose to move on with their life.

Many combat veterans continue to grieve the loss of their friends and other losses incurred through wartime trauma because they have never fully reached reconciliation.

ADDRESSING GRIEF

One's capacity to successfully deal with grief is often enhanced by the presence of a dynamic and sensitive network of caring people— family, friends, or a supportive congregation. The grieving person's ability to reach reconciliation, while individually determined, will ultimately depend upon their willingness to live with loss, cope with pain, and move on with life.

Healing from the wound of grief depends upon the grieving person's willingness to talk about their pain and, frankly, the willingness of others to listen. Too frequently, others dismiss the grieving person's loss too soon: *It's time to move on; you need to get over your loss.* But the numerous aspects of loss make the healing process complicated. How do you tell a servicemember who has lost his legs or his friends *You need to get over your losses and move on*? How do you tell a grieving spouse *You'll have to learn to cope without your spouse and raise your children without that parent*? You don't.

The first step—and perhaps the most important—is to grant the victim permission to grieve. Sometimes people feel like they don't deserve to grieve. But we must affirm their loss and allow for grief, or in some cases, honor a person's reasons for grieving. Encourage the grieving person to talk about pain and loss. "Pain shared is pain divided." Allowing for verbal expression enables the mourner to acknowledge grief, identify fears, and focus on assets, not just losses.

It may be helpful to ask *Are you able to identify any resources that you can use to get through this time of loss?* It's not unusual for victims to feel like they have absolutely no resources available to them. They may feel like their lives are ruined and that there is no reason to go on. When grieving people are able to identify and access their resources, they are learning to cope with their loss.

It's normal for those who grieve to feel ambivalent about their choices. They may feel like their lives are out of control. One can help by assisting in reestablishing their routines and encouraging them to engage in healthy activities.

The stress of the grief experience turns the mourner's world upside down. Gaining control mitigates the level of stress. Focusing grieving energy on constructive activities like prayer and goal-setting helps the grieving person. This is what Nehemiah did. He also found his strength in God's comfort. By doing this, the grieving person gains perspective and realizes more quickly the things they can and cannot change. This realization gives new perspective on the loss. Also, time and distance aid the healing process.

NOTES

1. Author's interview with CSM James Carabello, US Army, 1-32 Infantry Regiment, 10th Mountain Division, Fort Drum, NY, April 2008.

2. Eugene B. Sledge, *With the Old Breed at Peleliu and Okinawa* (New York: Presidio Press, 2007), 140, 141.

3. Matsakis, Post-traumatic.

4. Alan Wolfelt, *Companioning the Bereaved: A Soulful Guide for Caregivers* (Fort Collins, CO: Companion Press, 2006).

5. John James and Russell Friedman, *The Grief Recovery Handbook*, rev. ed. (New York: Harper Perennial, 1998).

6. K. Tolstikova, S. Fleming, and B. Chartier, "Grief, Complicated Grief, and Trauma: The Role of the Search for Meaning, Impaired Self-Reference, and Death Anxiety," *Illness, Crisis & Loss* 13 (2005): 293–313.

7. K. J. Doka, *Disenfranchised Grief: New Directions, Challenges, and Strategies for Practice* (Champaign, IL: Research Press, 2002).

8. Hoge, *Once a Warrior*.

9. See Dave Grossman, *On Killing: The Psychological Cost of Learning to Kill in War and Society* (New York: Back Bay Books, 1996).

10. Dewey, *War and Redemption*.

11. Ibid. See also Meichenbaum, *A Clinical Handbook*; Shay, *Achilles in Vietnam*.

12. Matsakis, *Post-traumatic*. See also "The Dominant Grief Symptom," *The Centre for the Grief Journey*, accessed December 27, 2015, http://www.griefjourney.com/wp/what-we-offer/for-professionals-and-caregivers/articles-for-professionals-and-caregivers/the-dominant-grief-symptom/.

13. Matsakis, *Post-traumatic*.

14. Granger E. Westberg, *Good Grief* (Minneapolis: Fortress Press, 1962).

15. Wolfelt, *Companioning the Bereaved*.

16. James and Friedman, *The Grief Recovery Handbook*.

17. Wolfelt, *Companioning the Bereaved*, 127.

18. Ibid.

19. See Shay, *Achilles in Vietnam*; Dewey, *War and Redemption*; Matsakis, *Back From the Front: Combat Trauma, Love, and the Family* (Baltimore: Sidran Institute Press, 2007); and Tick, *War and the Soul*.

20. Bonura, "A Biblical Approach."

21. Matsakis, *Post-traumatic*.

22. Wolfelt, *Companioning the Bereaved*.

23. Ibid.

24. Ibid.

25. Fuller-Rogers, *Pastoral Care*; Matsakis, *Post-traumatic*.

26. Wolfelt, *Companioning the Bereaved*; Matsakis, *Post-traumatic*.

27. Fuller-Rogers, *Pastoral Care*; Wolfelt, *Companioning the Bereaved*.

28. Wolfelt, *Companioning the Bereaved*.

29. Ibid.

30. J. Glenn Gray, *The Warriors: Reflections of Men in Battle* (Lincoln, NE: University of Nebraska Press, 1970), 51.

31. Ibid., 52.

32. Author's interview with CSM James Carabello, April 2008.

33. Sledge, *With the Old Breed*.

34. Matsakis, *Post-traumatic*.

35. Ibid.

36. Sarah A. Haley, "When the Patient Reports Atrocities: Specific Treatment Considerations of the Vietnam Veteran," *Archives of General Psychiatry* 30 (1974): 191–196.

37. Wolfelt, *Companioning the Bereaved*.

38. Ibid.

39. Ibid. See also Herman, *Trauma and Recovery*.

40. Wolfelt, *Companioning the Bereaved*.

41. Fuller-Rogers, *Pastoral Care*; Wolfelt, *Companioning the Bereaved*.

42. Wolfelt, *Companioning the Bereaved*.

43. J. William Worden, *Grief Counseling and Grief Therapy: A Handbook for the Mental Health Practitioner* (New York: Springer, 1991); Wolfelt, *Companioning the Bereaved*.

CHAPTER 4

FORMS OF LOSS ASSOCIATED WITH GRIEF

Mostly it is loss which teaches us about the worth of things.

—Arthur Schopenhauer,
Pererga and Paralipomena

THE 1946 motion picture *The Best Years of Our Lives* tells the story of three returning World War II veterans: a Soldier, an Airman, and a Sailor, each from a different station of society, who struggle to regain their lives after the war. We're first introduced to Al Stephenson. Before the war he was a banker and a family man with a wife and a couple of children. An older man compared to the typical veteran, Al returns to discover his daughters are now adults and his wife has changed. Faced with the challenges of reestablishing his banking position and renewing his relationships with his family, he realizes he has lost the familiarity and intimacy that he once enjoyed with his family. He's like a stranger to them, and he finds it difficult to fit in.

Then there is Fred Derry, an airman who served as a bombardier in the European theater. He returns to civilian life with no meaningful job prospects or career plans. So he takes a job at a pharmacy and works at the snack counter. He struggles to find meaningful work; additionally, he's faced with the realization that the woman he married during flight training is not the woman he really loves, and the feeling is mutual. It's like he's lost everything, career and marriage, and has to start all over.

Lastly, there is Homer Parrish, who lost both his hands in a shipboard fire. He appears to cope fairly well and has learned to use his prosthetic hooks adeptly. But he suffers from the loss of esteem and feels unworthy of the love of his childhood sweetheart. He feels he would only be a burden to her. His loss is the physical loss of limbs that contributes to other perceived losses—the loss of self-esteem and of his sweetheart.

TANGIBLE AND INTANGIBLE LOSSES

Servicemembers suffer many losses in combat. And warriors always grieve their losses, particularly the loss of fellow warriors. While they may sometimes suffer the loss of life or limb or possessions, they almost always suffer an intangible loss. They may lose their confidence, sense of control, power, opportunities, or personal dignity.[1] These are powerful aspects of grief and may include other losses such as loss of identity, innocence, peace, faith, meaning, and community.[2] These may be losses about who the servicemember is or what they long to be.

While no tangible or intangible loss can be completely separated from another, such as the loss of a limb from social or economic loss, some losses are more directly related to spirituality. Among these are loss of identity, loss of faith, loss of peace, loss of meaning, and feelings of alienation, isolation, and loneliness—all of which might also be called existential losses. They are really inseparable and often intertwined with other issues, such as anger, guilt and shame. In the sections below, I'll describe some of the losses that are more directly related to spirituality.

Loss of Identity and the Problem of Dissociation

Loss of identity has to do with changes in the way warriors perceive themselves and the world around them.[3] An individual's capacity for reason, conscience, personal choice, or aesthetic sensibility, including imagination and intimacy, are so deeply affected by trauma that their identity is damaged or distorted. Sufferers lose touch with themselves or with their moral bearings: they have difficulty distinguishing between right and wrong.

In severe cases, loss of identity is associated with the psychological state of dissociation, in which thoughts, emotions, identity, and memory are not integrated within a person.[4]

Identity dysfunction is manifested by social dysfunction, expressed by the inability to experience pleasure or show interest in anything. The problem stems from the warfighter's inability to integrate a traumatic experience into their life—that is, to assign meaning to it or make sense of it.

Servicemembers who suffer from dissociation seem detached; they feel like they're living in a slow-motion dream or in a world where they are outside of themselves. Everything seems distorted and unreal.

In severe trauma cases, there is a significant disintegration. The subconscious brain cannot let go of the trauma, and there is a disruption of normal neural functions. Dissociation compensates for this severe disruption through intrapersonal detachment, sometimes described not only as being separated from oneself but also as severe emotional numbing.

Dissociation may function as a self-preservation measure against pain, fear, helplessness, and panic. It enables detachment from the physical trauma, memory of the trauma, and those associated with the event. Dissociation is an extreme manifestation of PTSD; it's not typical of those who suffer from combat-related PTSD.

Trauma does not necessarily lead to an identity crisis or dissociation. But the development of PTS usually negatively affects perceptions of self and the community. Such negative perceptions may lead to other issues, such as disillusionment, depression, withdrawal, and suicide.

As one example, a Soldier witnessed an IED attack on a convoy of vehicles that was passing in front of his post. A vehicle directly in front of him was hit setting it on fire. Unable to leave his position, he was left to watch the vehicle burn and listen to the screams of the Soldiers who were trapped inside. Others in the convoy attempted to rescue the trapped Soldiers, but they failed. This servicemember may struggle with identity issues or suffer with PTSD because he was unable to help in the situation. He may feel responsible for contributing to his comrades' deaths. His mind may replay the sights and sounds of that day. Such disruptions would profoundly affect the way he sees himself and contribute to loss of identity and sense of self.

We know that loss of identity degrades competency and is almost always attended by perceptions of personal failure, lack of emotional control, and inability to regulate one's self appropriately. It's not difficult, then, to see how loss of identity is closely associated with the experience of guilt and shame. Furthermore, the presence of identity loss coupled with other losses complicates grief, making it much more difficult to achieve reconciliation or normalization.

In extreme traumatic cases, such as with prisoners of war (POWs), stress is usually equally extreme, attended by deprivation, dehumanization, and torture, to an extent that the victim experiences a kind of mental death—or, as others have observed, a "soul death."[5] I've never observed this, but former POWs have. They tell me that POWs enduring soul death frequently didn't survive, having lost the will to live. This extreme effect of trauma is often associated with alienation, distrust, shame, and guilt.[6]

LOSS OF INNOCENCE

In Harper Lee's Pulitzer Prize-winning classic *To Kill a Mockingbird*, Atticus's children gradually learn the world is harsh and full of prejudice. It's also a cruel and unforgiving world. The loss of innocence is the realization that the world does not operate according to one's earlier assumptions. It is the sudden or gradual initiation into reality—the way the world really operates, the way the world is. It's a world in which there are no simple answers. War typically immerses the uninitiated into the reality of pain, sorrow, fear, and confusion.

In Erich M. Remarque's novel *The Road Back*, the main character, Ernst, who has just returned from the Great War, mutters profanity in the presence of his mother. She has never heard him use vulgar language and is shocked. Combat has changed Ernst. He's no longer the innocent son she once knew. He has seen and done terrible things, unmentionable things that were fueled by panic and rage, which left him nauseated and disgusted with himself.[7]

The loss of innocence not only involves changes in expression and exposure to horrible things, it often develops into cynicism. It's a realization that war is not what the servicemember originally believed it to be, like some kind of great adventure. War is far from that. The loss of innocence may result in reckless behavior, a carelessness that defies rationalization, manifested in ways like reckless driving, abuse of alcohol or drugs, and even violence and criminal activity.

But it's also possible for the loss of innocence to lead to a mature, realistic view of the world and produce positive changes, like a desire to serve humanity in some constructive fashion, to make a positive difference for others. Some veterans report commitments they made in combat: if they survived, they would serve their fellow man in redeeming ways. So the loss of innocence sometimes leads to personal actualization.

PERSONALITY CHANGES

Exposure to combat may result in serious personality changes. These personality changes can represent a loss. I've met with several Soldiers who indicated radical changes in their personalities after returning from combat. One of these Soldiers was a Christian and deeply committed to the Lord. He enjoyed assisting in worship services and serving in other capacities when he was overseas. But during his time in the war zone, he became disturbed by the loss of life and the troubles in his unit. He felt demeaned by others and even betrayed by his leadership. All of these things radically affected his personality and brought about a lot of frustration, anger, and despair. He admitted that he had become a different person.

I counseled another servicemember who was being treated for traumatic brain injury and PTSD. The Soldier's wartime experience had completely changed him. Unable to concentrate, complete multiple tasks, and generally function as he once did, he became withdrawn, deliberate, and cautious, handling tasks one at a time. His brain no longer worked as it used to because of the brain injury, a problem further complicated by the symptoms of combat-related PTSD. Family members were unable to relate to him as they used to, and as a result he felt alone and misunderstood. But he has been working hard at getting his life back together and refuses to accept defeat. He's reached out to others with similar challenges and has been a help to them.

There are other stories not as promising. One Soldier reported that his whole personality changed after he came back from the war. He lost his friends because they could not cope with his PTSD. He became suspicious of others and withdrawn. He was plagued by feelings of worthlessness. His PTSD devastated his life and changed him completely from the confident man he once was to a man who was uncertain about the future and confused about the present.

Sadly, many veterans are floundering in a kind of post-trauma malaise, unable to find their way out of their pain or get their lives back on track. Others are having some success—servicemembers who refuse to be defeated by their experience or defined by their trauma.

Loss of Peace

Frequently, the manifestation of trauma symptoms creates an inner turbulence that might be identified as a loss of peace. The loss of peace occurs at multiple levels—relational, personal, and spiritual. Servicemembers who are struggling to reintegrate into life and constantly encountering intrusive symptoms are not at peace. They usually experience intense inner conflict. They're also often in conflict with the people closest to them. Their world has turned upside down. Many are in a downward spiral, unable to extract themselves and unable to achieve any sense of balance.

These warriors have strained relationships, and sometimes the strain is manifested in violence. The inability of the warrior to talk about his or her experience inhibits familial relationships and contributes to a sense of alienation in the home. The problem of the warfighter is the "elephant in the room" and family members usually feel like they have to "walk on eggshells" just to keep the peace. The "problem" is rarely discussed for fear the servicemember will react violently or slip further into depression. Servicemembers who suffer from guilt or grief may subject themselves to a conscious replaying of the trauma incident and question themselves and their actions. PTS often includes insomnia, which contributes to this loss of inner peace.

Many traumatized servicemembers suffer spiritually. They find themselves at odds with God and with people of faith. They find it difficult to reconnect with their faith, often feeling unworthy of God's love or his forgiveness. Having no peace *with* God, they lack the peace *of* God, feeling anxious, worried, and fearful. Frequently the loss of peace is attended by feelings of hopelessness and despair. Warriors without God's peace feel abandoned by God. Desiring to find God, they are so bereft and alone they do not even know where to begin.

Loss of Faith

Traumatic events such as war frequently challenge core beliefs—not only beliefs about how the world should work or about what is good and true, but belief in God. Loss of faith usually manifests as a violation of what is sacred to the person.[8] Loss of faith, compounded by feelings of divine abandonment and even betrayal, is not uncommon among combat veterans.

For some, the experience of trauma is a crisis of faith, a dilemma from which there is no apparent escape. It may evoke feelings that God is responsible in some way for their trauma. It may lead victims to conclude that they do not deserve God's mercy, forgiveness, or peace. Some feel doomed and cast off forever from God because of their wartime actions.

Army Chaplain Roger Benimoff temporarily lost his faith after two deployments to Iraq.[9] Perhaps a victim of too much grief, Chaplain Benimoff questioned the love of God. His case is not unusual, but when the chaplain has doubts, then many others are affected. The heart of deep compassion is often vulnerable to breakage. The pain is common among chaplains and other caregivers who have seen their servicemembers die or who have cared for the dead. I served with a colleague who was deeply affected by the loss of a little girl who was mortally wounded in Iraq. Add to this the various other stresses servicemembers face—separation from family, marital troubles, and problems with teenage children causing additional grief for the single parent at home—and eventually these things take their toll.

Loss of faith is especially egregious because of the perception that somehow God failed the individual. Spiritual values and religious beliefs are entrenched. These are matters of the soul. If one's theological system fails to account for death, violence, and war, then it will prove inadequate and lead to a crisis of belief. This spiritual tension always exists for people of faith.

The problem of evil is an age-old theological dilemma. It contributes to the loss of faith among some warriors who have seen the effects of war. Being able to accommodate the reality of war—the facts that innocent people die and friends are lost—is essential for keeping a servicemember's faith intact. One must possess a theology that adequately accounts for the presence of evil and the suffering of the innocent.

I lost friends in Iraq. First Sergeant Aaron Jagger and I served together in OIF I. After we returned to Germany, we established a coffeehouse program as an outreach to our Soldiers. He was an outstanding, talented musician and popular with the Soldiers.

On August 9, 2006, on his second deployment to Iraq, he was violently killed near Ramadi by a huge roadside bomb. Soldiers in his unit were deeply affected, as well as family members back home, as you might imagine. The loss of any servicemember, especially a popular leader, hurts morale and impacts unit cohesion. It's easy to lose mission focus, and it takes time to recover. I learned about his death much later, and hearing the news renewed a cycle of grief for me.

Aaron's loss left a big hole in our lives. How do we deal with such painful losses? Losses like this are deeply felt and not easily reconciled. One could easily blame God. And often we're left with the question: *Why?*

Chaplain Benimoff was not the first believer to question the love of God when facing traumatic circumstances; he was not the first to grieve the loss of comrades-in-arms and certainly not the last. Nevertheless, his grief was apparently real; and it led to a temporary loss of faith.*

When faced with the challenge of reconciling the way the world is with what they believe, people either find a way to accommodate the challenge or cast off the discordant belief altogether. Loss of faith is about the inability to accommodate horrible, inexplicable events. The loss of life, especially innocent life, that comes with war can be overwhelming. Some abandon the ship of faith, unable to reconcile it with their combat experiences. But many others find strength and encouragement from their faith and are not derailed by the trauma they encounter.

---

* Chaplain Benimoff found his faith again and currently works as an advisor and counselor on veterans' issues.

For example, one of my Soldiers gave his life to Christ because of his combat experience. In my discussions with Soldiers, I've found many returned from combat strengthened by their faith or renewed in their spiritual outlook. Some reported important spiritual decisions that were made in combat; still, others returned from combat with a greater sense of spiritual commitment to God.

Combat presents problems about killing. Killing is a severe and inhuman act. Despite the validity of distinctions between wartime killing and murder, such distinctions do not make killing any easier for most warriors. In war there is usually a tremendous loss of innocent life, sometimes characterized as collateral damage. It's often difficult to reconcile not only the killing of legitimate combatants but also the sad and unfortunate killing of innocent people with one's religious beliefs.

In certain types of traumatic events, like war, an individual can be both victim and perpetrator of trauma. Warriors in combat situations can be either exposed to the injury and death of others or wounded themselves, and simultaneously directly involved in killing. These realities may cause a warfighter to question his or her role in war and lead to a crisis of faith.

It's possible for core elements of a person's worldview—for example, patriotism and faith—to be in conflict, creating doubt and uncertainty about the right course of action. Subsequent spiritual questioning not only results in loss of faith but may increase guilt or self-blame, contributing to alienation from others or from God.

Individuals may experience a disconnection between the beliefs they were raised with, their expectations about what military service would be like, and actual war zone experiences.

Tragically, those who lose faith in God also lose faith with their communities and authorities—religious, military, social, or political.[10] Servicemembers may lose faith in "the cause," wondering if the war is worth the suffering and dying. I met Soldiers who joined the Army after 9/11 because they loved their country. They joined because they wanted to defend the American way of life, they wanted to promote freedom—they wanted to do their part! But along the way, they came to realize the war was a lot more complicated than they had originally thought. The loss of friends, and such things as the restrictive application of the ROE, led to cynicism and questions about how the U.S. military was conducting the war.

It is the responsibility of military and political leaders to communicate the purpose and desired end state of any military operation. A failure on their part to clarify the mission can contribute to a warrior's loss of faith.

Clergy have a huge responsibility here. We must address loss of faith and make every effort to bring these lost souls back into the fold. This can be accomplished through small and loving groups who develop ways to reach out to our veterans, providing a safe and secure environment where love, trust, and faith are strengthened and hope is renewed.

LOSS OF MEANING

Making sense of one's pain is central to healing for victims of trauma, and conventional therapies do not adequately address this issue.[11] Loss of meaning is almost always associated with combat-related trauma and is especially egregious for combat veterans; many of whom suffer with a sense of persistent meaninglessness for years.[12] Their struggle to make sense of trauma makes it difficult for them to comprehend God's love or derive any positive meaning in their lives.[13] Combat veterans want to know their wartime service counts for something: that it has some redemptive value or that the loss of life was worth the price.

The true account of Ernest Gordon, portrayed in the motion picture *To End All Wars*, provides insight into the matter of meaning and loss. The story is about four Allied POWs who endured harsh treatment from their Japanese captors during World War II while being forced to build a railroad through the Thai-Burmese jungle. Beaten, starved, and stripped of almost everything but their dignity, the men struggled to find meaning and purpose in their horrid existence.

Severe trauma such as Gordon and other POWs experienced in the jungles of Burma calls into question the meaning and purpose of life. A sufferer's search for meaning generates huge amounts of existential anxiety. Failure to assign meaning to a traumatic experience risks sending the sufferer further and further on a spiraling, downward path to meaninglessness and total despair.[14]

A need for meaning was certainly felt by many POWs who were enslaved by the Japanese during World War II. Fortunately, through the leadership of Gordon and others and despite their brutal existence, some were able to discover meaning in their pain and, thus, were able to cope with their situation.

The task of the pastoral caregiver is to assist the sufferer in finding meaning behind the pain. When victims discover the meaning for their pain, it becomes less difficult for them to integrate the trauma into their lives. Making meaning is the first step to healing. Failure to integrate the traumatic experience is usually failure to find the meaning of the pain.

On a larger scale, the "will to meaning," or the need to make meaning of life, is a universal quest. It is suffering that often brings this quest to the level of human consciousness. Viktor Frankl, among others, has helped us understand our need to find meaning in our existence and particularly in our suffering. A Holocaust survivor,

Frankl learned the lessons of suffering by observing the behavior of others in the Nazi death camps during World War II. Losing family and friends, he found himself stripped of everything but his capacity to choose. Our human capacity to choose our attitude is what he called "the last of the human freedoms."[15] When we exercise our capacity to choose, we retain our humanity and our dignity. That's how we survive, and that's how we find meaning. It was in that choosing, he observed, that people made their lives "meaningful and purposeful."[16]

To suffer bravely, Frankl argued, is to embrace one's suffering and claim meaning in that suffering. The very act of embracing the pain makes us human and preserves our dignity. It is an act of meaning. When faced with the intractable and inescapable circumstances of an Auschwitz or some other horrible experience, "suffering ceases to be suffering in some way at the moment it finds a meaning, such as the meaning of a sacrifice," Frankl observed.[17]

Toward the end, while others wondered if they might survive the camp and thereby find meaning in their suffering, Frankl concluded differently: "Has all this suffering, this dying around us, a meaning? For, if not, then ultimately there is no meaning to survival; for a life whose meaning depends upon such happenstance—whether one escapes or not—ultimately would not be worth living at all."[18]

The will to meaning is a powerful motivation for those who suffer a traumatic event, especially an event that resulted in a severe grief reaction. Since grief is a primary symptom of combat-related PTS, the need to make meaning out of trauma is paramount. Moreover, failure to find meaning complicates grief, making it more difficult to come to reconciliation with loss.

In studies conducted by Alan Fontana and Robert Rosenheck, reported in the *Journal of Nervous and Mental Disease*, veterans faced with a high loss of meaning preferred to talk to clergy, versus veterans with a low loss of meaning who felt no need to explore their sense of loss with clergy. These studies revealed clergy were best equipped to address existential issues such as loss of meaning.[19] Given this finding and the significance of meaning loss, clergy have a critical role in leading those who suffer from a loss of meaning to a place of meaning, hope, and healing.

The Loss of Community

The loss of community is the warrior's inability to reconnect to friends, family, and associates. It is another form of alienation. Loss of community is aggravated by the fact that civilians do not understand or share the warrior's experience. This is understandable. Soldiers are often reluctant to tell their stories. So barriers naturally exist between the combat veteran and a typical civilian community.

In *The Road Back*, the character Ludwig Breyer has just returned from his wartime service in France during the Great War. He is a student at a teachers' college and tries to explain to his professor how the civilian view of war is radically different from the service-member's perspective:

> [Y]ou have seen the war after your fashion—with flying banners, martial music, and with glamour. But you saw it only to the railway station from which we set off. —We do not mean to blame you. We, too, thought as you did. But we have seen the other side since then, and against that the heroics of 1914 soon wilted to nothing. Yet we went through with it—we went through with it because there was something deeper that held us together, something that only showed up out there, a responsibility perhaps, but at any rate something of which you know nothing and about which there can be no speech.[20]

An important first step for those in the civilian community is to recognize that a barrier exists between the veteran and civilian communities. Most civilians do not know what it means to serve as a warrior, but they can listen and learn. This takes time, patience, and skill. Unfortunately, the loss of community further contributes to the warrior's sense of alienation and isolation.

Pastoral caregivers are faced with the important challenge of relating effectively to returning veterans who are struggling to reconnect with their churches. While most veterans are not quick to share their stories or questions, clergy must be prepared to respond appropriately by demonstrating a desire to understand. Many returning servicemembers report difficulty reuniting with their churches, getting back to where they were before they left for war.[21] These veterans are struggling with their actions in combat and with the things they saw. They want to know that God accepts them and he is there for them. If they are not able to reconnect with the community, especially with their faith community, they will be lost.

Clergy can reach out to veterans by going to them, visiting with them at the VA, attending and supporting military-focused events in the community, and collaborating with veterans already in their churches to reach veterans outside of their churches. It takes time and resources, but it's not impossible.

Veterans need to know you really care. As Theodore Roosevelt said, "People don't care how much you know until they know how much you care." Putting on a seminar for veterans in your community without building the necessary groundwork and rapport is usually not effective. Veterans respond to genuine, sincere, tangible actions. It is better to search out the veteran, like the shepherd who left the ninety-nine to look after the one, than to stage a rally or a big seminar and expect veterans to show up.

Loss of community is significant because healing is only found in community. Society's caregivers must somehow bridge the chasm that exists between the civilian community and the warrior community and try to understand the warrior's sense of responsibility that exists in the combat zone. Servicemembers suffering from PTS desperately need the safety and security of a supportive community. Typically, this community is the brotherhood of arms. But society must also step in and serve as a healing community, provided the community is equipped with knowledge, skills, and emotional capacity to enter into the warrior's story.

ALIENATION, ISOLATION, AND LONELINESS

The experience of alienation, isolation, and loneliness is an expression of loss and part of the grieving process. Alienation is the feeling of being apart and alone. It is a feeling of not being understood. Isolation is the inability to feel affection or form close relationships. It is the result of alienation. Loneliness is the absence of companionship and is usually accompanied by feelings of sadness.

In the motion picture *Gran Torino*, the plot revolves around the experience of widower Walt Kowalski, played by Clint Eastwood. Walt, a retired autoworker and Korean War veteran who received the Silver Star medal for gallantry in combat, is a grumpy and embittered old man who cannot get along with his adult children or his Hmong neighbors. When Thao, a Hmong teenager who lives next door, is pressured by the neighborhood gang to steal Walt's pristine, 1972 Gran Torino, Walt goes into an angry tirade, threatening Thao with bodily harm and demanding that Thao's family leave him alone.

But a friendship develops despite what Thao did. Eventually Walt is drawn into the life of this family and feels compelled to defend them from the gang that terrorizes the neighborhood.

Underlying this script is the nagging reality of Walt's wartime service in Korea. There are enduring effects from the trauma he experienced by taking human life, losing his friends, and more recently losing his wife. While the plot reflects the negative effects of war-related and other trauma, it most poignantly shows us the withdrawal, isolation, and loneliness of one who continues to suffer many years later.

The movie also depicts Walt's alienation from the church, his family, and his friends. The parish priest often visits Walt, but his visits are rebuffed. Walt's sense of shame and unworthiness is clearly evident in the story, from which he ultimately finds redemption.

Many warriors returning today from Iraq and Afghanistan suffer from feelings of alienation and isolation, just like Walt. They find it difficult to reconnect to loved ones, friends, and acquaintances. War has changed them. War changes everyone.

In *The Road Back*, Ernst reveals that his feelings of loneliness and isolation hinder him from reintegrating into civilian society. The comradeship he enjoyed at the front with members of his platoon is gone. Now he, along with his comrades, drifts in a kind of netherworld between the life they lived at the front and life back home. They struggle to relate to members of the civilian community. They struggle to find their place.

The sentiment so accurately captured by Remarque is real and typical of veterans, who struggle with their return to society. Servicemembers suffering like this tell me they would much rather go back to Iraq or Afghanistan than remain in a society where it is so difficult to readjust. They long for the comradeship and simplicity of life in the combat zone, despite the danger.

Why is readjusting to civilian society so difficult for warriors? The intrusive memories of wartime trauma disrupted their ability to function. The frequent intrusiveness of the trauma interferes with social, familial, and occupational functioning. The coping skills they used in combat do not work for them back home. Indeed, such battle skills work against them. Lingering hypervigilant reactions necessary in combat are out of place back home. The distrust and suspicion honed in combat contribute to distrust toward civilians and even family members away from the combat zone. Such patterns, necessary in combat, are sometimes difficult to change. They may continue involuntarily.

The problem of intrusion contributes to alienation by fueling avoidance habits. Some sights and sounds trigger trauma reactions, so servicemembers may avoid shopping malls or churches because crowds make them feel unsafe and trigger intrusive memories. Such memories are painful, and warriors further isolate themselves to escape the pain. Civilians who do not understand this reaction may appear insensitive, and servicemembers may feel angry toward them because of the perceived insensitivity. Some servicemembers will suppress their anger. Others will vent it in road rage or domestic violence, further alienating themselves from society.

A sense of alienation is also evident among victims of rape. A study of rape victims reported feelings of internal and social alienation. Victims felt estranged from their futures, unable to picture futures for themselves. Experiences that contributed to their overall sense of alienation included being blamed, being mistreated, or not being believed. Their sense of alienation was deepened by an inability to relate to others after the trauma or by sensing others did not meet their needs. Their reactions were not very different from those of veterans who struggle with PTS. While the nature of the trauma is different, the alienation and feelings of isolation are much the same.

In cases where rape victims were able to relate their experiences in a safe and supported environment, feelings of alienation lessened. Similarly, where veterans are able to share their experiences in a safe and secure environment, feelings of alienation diminish. This outcome is similar to what Brené Brown discovered regarding shame among rape victims. Higher ratings of feelings of alienation were present where perceptions of support decreased.[22]

Isolation and social withdrawal may inhibit one's connection to the sacred, one's relationship to God. In interviews I did with veterans, most Soldiers were incapable of feeling connected to God but still professed their belief in him. Others expressed a lack of interest in participating in religious communities, although they frequently prayed.

Researchers tell us that feelings of loneliness are among the most common emotional symptoms and a frequent source of human suffering.[23] Loneliness is no discriminator against race, gender, or creed. Just about everybody suffers from loneliness at one time or another. It's a universal condition characterized by an inner, painful emptiness. Sociologist Robert Weiss has estimated that a quarter of the American population suffers from loneliness at some time during any given month.[24]

Combat veterans are highly vulnerable to loneliness, especially those who are suffering from severe traumatic effects. They find themselves isolated from family and friends, unable to explain their feelings or their experiences. As their condition worsens, their loneliness increases. They withdraw into themselves. Feelings of emptiness deepen. Intimacy becomes nonexistent. Normal interaction with neighbors or associates becomes strained and unnatural. No one seems to understand; no one seems to care. Lonely veterans feel rejected and unwanted. These victims drive themselves into an abyss of total isolation.

Such a devolving sense of loneliness only contributes to feelings of utter worthlessness and uselessness. Servicemembers suffering in this way continue to feel isolated and misunderstood. Attempts by others to connect with them are often rebuffed, leading to further isolation.

Lonely people blame themselves for their loneliness, and they may become angry with themselves. Their anger pushes people away. Angry people feel frustrated, perhaps because they are unable to express themselves. They feel angry because of perceived or real injustices. War produces many injustices and opportunities for betrayal. These actions often contribute to the fear and suspicion that are expressed as anger by victims of PTS.

The combined effects of PTS, including anger, frustration, guilt, grief, and shame, explain how easy it is for veterans to feel alienated, isolated, and lonely. But interaction with others is exactly what they need. They need to be accepted back into the community, where their stories can eventually be told and their persons understood, accepted, and embraced.

NOTES

1. Matsakis, *Post-traumatic*.
2. Fuller-Rogers, *Pastoral Care*; Matsakis, Post-traumatic; Herman, *Trauma and Recovery*.
3. Tick, *War and the Soul*; Herman, *Trauma and Recovery*.
4. Maryhelen Kreidler, Melissa Zupancic, Cynthia Bell, and Mary Beth Longo, "Trauma and Dissociation: Treatment Perspectives," *Perspectives in Psychiatric Care* 36 (2000): 77–85.
5. Ibid. See also Tick, *War and the Soul*.
6. C. R. Brewin, R. Garnett and B. Andrews, "Trauma, Identity and Mental Health in UK Military Veterans," *Psychological Medicine* 41 (2011): 1733–1740.
7. Remarque, *The Road Back*, 143.
8. Mahoney et al., "Broken Vows"; Fuller-Rogers, *Pastoral Care*.
9. Eve Conant, "Faith Under Fire," *Newsweek* (May 7, 2007): 26–34; see also Eve Conant, "God, War, and the Presidency," *Newsweek*, May 6, 2007, accessed January 10, 2016 http://www.newsweek.com/god-war-and-presidency-101397; Roger Benimoff, *Faith Under Fire: An Army Chaplain's Memoir* (New York: Crow Publishing Group, 2009).
10. Fuller-Rogers, *Pastoral Care*.
11. R. M. Gilmartin and S. Southwick, "Combat-Related PTSD and Logotherapy," International Forum for Logotherapy 27 (2004): 34–38, accessed March 6, 2009, http://www.ptsd.va.gov/professional/articles/article-pdf/id28635.pdf; Crystal L. Park and Amy L. Ai, "Making Meaning and Growth: New Directions for Research on Survivors of Trauma," *Journal of Loss and Trauma* 11 (2006): 389-407.
12. Lawrence G. Calhoun and Richard G. Tedeschi, *Facilitating Posttraumatic Growth: A Clinician's Guide* (Mahwah, NJ: Erlbaum, 1999); L. Decker, "The Role of Trauma in Spiritual Development," *Journal of Humanistic Psychology* 33, (1993): 33–46; R. Janoff-Bulman, *Shattered Assumptions: Towards a New Psychology of Trauma* (New York: Free Press, 1992); Robert Hicks, *Returning Home: Practical Advice for War Veterans, their Families and Friends* (Tarrytown, NY: Fleming H. Revell Co., 1991); Shay, *Achilles in Vietnam*.
13. Dewey, *War and Redemption*.
14. Paulson, "The Hard Issues."
15. Viktor Frankl, *Man's Search for Meaning: An Introduction to Logotherapy* (New York: Pocket Books, 1959), 104.
16. Ibid., 106.
17. Ibid., 179.
18. Ibid., 183.
19. Alan Fontana and Robert Rosenheck, "Trauma, Change in Strength of Religious Faith and Mental Health Service Use Among Veterans Treated for PTSD," *Journal of Nervous and Mental Disease* 192 (2004): 579–584.
20. Remarque, *The Road Back*, 125.

21. See "Spiritual Alienation," accessed December 21, 2015, http://www.ptsdsupport.net/spirit.html.

22. Brown, "Shame Resilience Theory."

23. Gary Collins, *Christian Counseling: A Comprehensive Guide*, rev. ed. (Nashville, TN: W Publishing Group, 1988).

24. Ibid.

CHAPTER 5

GUILT AND SHAME

In my mind, I murdered those people. I will never forgive myself and neither can God forgive me.

—A combat veteran

I N the movie *Bella*, a promising international soccer player is involved in an accident that results in the death of a child, the loss of a career, and a five-year prison sentence. The accident completely changes his life. The story portrays the man's guilt and shame as he comes to terms with the consequences of the accident. Through this experience, he learns new things about himself and its meaning for his life.

Servicemembers struggle with guilt and shame too. Psychologists and chaplains in Iraq formed trauma response teams and often encountered warriors who struggled with guilt and shame. In one incident, a Soldier who was recovering from a gunshot wound to the neck indicated he felt guilty and ashamed because he believed God was punishing him for sinful thoughts at the time he was wounded.[1]

Veterans who committed war atrocities, perceived or real, are also vulnerable. But they may numb themselves to these transgressions. I spoke to one veteran who admitted to committing an atrocity but felt no guilt or shame for what he did.

Servicemembers who survive horrific experiences often suffer from survivor's guilt. They may blame themselves for surviving and even sometimes feel that they should have died instead of their comrades. The problem of guilt or shame is pervasive among our returning veterans, and pastoral caregivers must be prepared to address these symptoms.

The act of killing creates challenges. Warfighters are trained to consider the enemy objectively, as a target that must be neutralized. It is not always necessary to neutralize the enemy, but when it is necessary, professional servicemembers view the act of killing dispassionately, as part of the business of warfighting. It requires a kind of desensitization. The consequences of this approach may have deeper spiritual implications. Such implications create difficulties for warriors, who may struggle to accept or reframe traumatic experiences, or find spiritual strength and meaning in them.

DISTINGUISHING GUILT AND SHAME

Guilt and shame are frequently associated with trauma and particularly with the onset of PTS. They represent major theological themes in Scripture. Guilt is often at the core of much human suffering and is a crucial factor in many problems people face.[2]

While guilt conveys a sense of responsibility or fault, shame has more to do with a personal sense of worthlessness. Guilt is about the failure to act or about acting inappropriately. Shame is about feeling bad because that is the way one perceives oneself.[3]

In *The Road Back*, Ernst returns home to learn that his friend Albert has suffered terribly from the war. He has lost both his feet. While there's nothing Ernst can do about it, the sight of his friend makes him feel ashamed and guilty. He cannot help but feel that he is to blame because he has his feet and Albert does not. This narrative illustrates how guilt is often linked to shame.

The same is true with the soccer player in the movie *Bella*. The soccer player, José, feels guilty because he was responsible for the car accident. He feels shame because he caused the death of a young child by his carelessness. He is ashamed because he believes his life has become worthless; and no matter what he does, he cannot redeem himself.

The focus of guilt is on conduct. Shame runs much deeper and has to do with character, which makes it much more difficult to experience improvement and well-being.[4] Shame is a consequence of wrongdoing, but not all people who feel shame are guilty of wrongdoing. Shame, like guilt, may be false when the feeling is based on false premises or misperceived wrongdoing. This was the case with Ernst. He had nothing to do with the loss of Albert's feet.

Guilt and shame may be indicators of a violated standard or a *perceived* violation. Caregivers must take the time to discover which one it is. Many servicemembers are blaming themselves for things they never did. Guilt and shame are essentially relational concepts, but guilt has a judicial aspect as well.[5]

Categories of Guilt

There are basically two categories of guilt: objective guilt and subjective guilt.[6] Objective guilt has to do with the violation of a standard whether legal, biblical, moral, personal, or societal. People can be objectively guilty regardless of how they feel.

Subjective guilt has to do with feelings. Feelings of guilt vary widely depending upon the standard that was violated. A violation of a personal standard, such as missing an exercise routine, is quite different from a violation of a legal or societal standard, such as robbing a bank. In every case of perceived guilt, counselors need to consider the subjective aspects of the guilt in relation to the violated standard.

Something may be legally acceptable but morally or ethically wrong. In this case, there is objective guilt based on a violation of a moral or ethical standard. Given the shifting values and standards of society, guilt is increasingly becoming a relative issue. Regardless, feelings of guilt are real and they must be addressed.

Subjective guilt is based entirely on feelings and personal perceptions of a violated standard. These perceptions may not always be accurate. So when considering aspects of guilt, both subjective and objective guilt must be examined.

Perceived Punishment and Guilt

Some veterans believe God is punishing them for their wartime actions and that forgiveness from God is unattainable. Certainly in cases where atrocities were committed, a servicemember would be objectively guilty before God. But regardless of the atrocity, God's forgiveness is always available to the violator. A problem arises when servicemembers are unable to forgive themselves and unable to accept the forgiveness of God. This is a subjective problem.

I once counseled a Soldier who suffered from immense guilt because of his actions in war. Those actions by any reasonable standard were not inappropriate. They involved killing, and he could not get over the fact that he had taken human life. He was never able to forgive himself for what he'd done, and he was convinced that God could never forgive him either.

His guilt was subjective because it was based on his feelings and personal perceptions. And it was real since it was his experience. But was it objectively valid? No. So far as I could tell, his actions did not violate the law of war nor any biblical or other moral standard.[7] But they obviously violated his personal standards, standards informed by his view of God and his understanding of war, which seemed to be skewed. Despite my reasoning with him, I could not convince him to change his views. He remained in his guilt, which I believed was really undeserved.

It is the task of the pastor or counselor to explore the problems of subjective guilt and perceived punishment from God, and point the client to the truths of Scripture. While the servicemember's guilt in my example was real and deeply felt, the more important issue for him was whether he could embrace God's forgiveness, forgive himself, and move on with his life. Unfortunately, it appeared that he became trapped in a self-condemning mind-set in which he made unequivocal determinations about himself and about God that were not necessarily deserved. God is always the answer to any kind of guilt. He is the one who can set us free from it.

THE BIBLICAL CONCEPT OF GUILT

The Old Testament concept of guilt is objective guilt. People were guilty because they transgressed the law of God. They might have acted without knowledge, yet, they were pronounced guilty all the same (Lev. 4:13–17; 5:17). Each person had the responsibility to make a ritual offering in obedience to God's commands. However, the offerings never removed the guilt of the people (Heb. 10:1–4). They only served as reminders of human frailty and shadows of a coming reality when, through Christ, the guilt of sin would be removed.[8]

Later in the Old Testament, the people fell under God's judgment and penalty for the sin of idolatry. In the prophetic writings, the focus of guilt was not only on the sin of idolatry but on failure to fulfill moral or ethical responsibilities, such as caring for orphans and widows or seeking justice and mercy (Mic. 6:8).

The Day of Atonement

On the Day of Atonement, the priest sacrificed an animal and placed its blood on the mercy seat, below the *Shekinah* glory of God's presence and above the law of God, which had been broken. A second animal was selected. The sins of the people were pronounced over it, and it was driven from the camp. It became the scapegoat and symbolized the removal of sin from God's people. But these provisions were only temporary and never removed sin.

The New Testament's Teaching on Guilt

In the New Testament, Jesus focused on the moral implications of guilt by addressing people's motives and challenging empty religiosity—outward deeds that had little relation to the moral responsibilities of fulfilling God's requirements (Luke 11:29–32; 12:47–48; 23:34).

Paul maintained being guilty meant the party was under the penalty of judgment (Rom. 3:19) or deserving punishment (1 Cor. 11:27; Jas. 2:10). A person was guilty because the individual had violated God's law (Jas. 2:10). However, Christ removed the guilt by the sacrifice of his own blood. By his blood, we have been cleansed from "an evil conscience," and we are no longer guilty before God (Heb. 10:21–22).

Christ fulfilled the will of the Father by becoming the acceptable, perfect, and willing sacrificial Lamb of God (John 1:20; Heb. 10:5–7). His sacrifice was perfect because it was sufficient and efficacious (Heb. 10:10–14). His sacrifice sanctified us; it set us apart unto God and brought us into God's family.[9]

VICTIM BLAME, FALSE GUILT, AND SURVIVOR'S GUILT

Servicemembers experience a sense of relief for surviving. This feeling of relief is normal but becomes problematic for many when they also feel guilty for surviving or guilty because they did not prevent the death of another.

Servicemembers naturally feel elated because they survived—*I'm glad it wasn't me.* But then they may feel guilty for that elation. In combat, death is everywhere, and warriors become calloused or numbed to it. Sometimes warriors feel guilty because of that callousness or because they do not grieve as they think they should. Unfortunately for some, the survival response that produces guilt may lead to shame—*I wish it had been me.*

The sense of failure is a common reaction among PTSD sufferers and is often experienced as "victim blame."[10] Some servicemembers blame themselves for what they perceive as an unforgivable violation. It is a guilt based on false premises. This is sometimes referred to as *false guilt.* Some servicemembers manifest false guilt by feeling unjustifiably responsible for the death of a comrade. It's not uncommon; indeed, I've dealt with several Soldiers struggling with their sense of responsibility and feelings of guilt for this very reason. They lost one of their Soldiers and they blame themselves, contrary to the facts.

Undeserved guilt is a problem particularly with leaders who have responsibility for servicemembers in combat. No military operation is ever executed flawlessly. Things always go wrong. While leaders must ultimately accept responsibility for their actions, it does not mean they have to blame themselves and bear the guilt for the loss of their servicemembers. But this is a hard thing for most leaders, and they often carry a heavy burden.

False guilt or self-blame is similar to survivor's guilt, in which the survivor laments, "Why did I live and my friend die?" Or they say, "If only I had done something differently, they would have lived." Such expressions have a negative impact on emotions and behavior. Servicemembers riddled with *false guilt* or self-blame suffer from cognitive distortions. It is a futile exercise that consumes one's energy and doesn't change anything in the end.

An example of false guilt, survivor's guilt, and victim blame comes to mind from Scripture in the story of Absalom. David is informed of Absalom's death. He blames himself, saying, "O my son Absalom, my son, my son Absalom! Would I had died instead of you, O Absalom, my son, my son!" (2 Sam. 18:33) While we acknowledge David's genuine grief, Absalom brought his death upon himself. He led the conspiracy against his father; he was to blame for his own death. Regardless, the perceived guilt and inward blame, as expressed by David, are real for some veterans and must be addressed. Indeed, later in the story, Joab, his commander, addresses it by rebuking David for blaming himself (2 Sam. 19:1–8).

JUSTIFIED GUILT

Justified guilt is a violation of an objective standard. Some veterans are justifiably guilty whether they acknowledge it or not. They may suffer from its effects whether they admit it or not. A veteran once told me that he had to drive through a crowd of people, likely injuring them, because he was told that he could not stop for anything. He displayed little or no remorse. It was just part of the job, an unfortunate occurrence in war. But he was guilty whether he acknowledged it or not. Servicemembers who commit war atrocities are justifiably guilty, and many of them suffer from the effects of PTS.

LABELS AND EPITAPHS

Labels such as "baby killers," epitaphs like "blood for oil," or general political statements about the morality of a particular war may contribute indirectly to a sense of guilt among PTS victims.[11] Society sometimes contributes to the guilt veterans feel by its failure to validate veterans or affirm veterans' roles in doing the dirty work of war. This was certainly the case with our Vietnam veterans. Our nation paid a dear price for its failure to affirm our veterans. All of these aspects of guilt represent spiritual and moral injuries—wounds to the soul that leave the sufferer in pain.

PATIENCE AND COMPASSION

Servicemembers who have received forgiveness for their sins may still feel guilty.[12] Care must be taken to bring the objective truths of Scripture before the sufferer in a way that demonstrates patience and compassion. In time, the subjective feelings of guilt will give way to the objective reality of God's Word. On one hand, it requires faith on the part of the believer; on the other hand, it requires the help of the Holy Spirit to apply the truths of Scripture to the believer's heart.

PERSONAL GUILT

Subjectively, humanity experiences feelings of guilt as a function of conscience, upbringing, or social and religious values. This aspect of subjective guilt is sometimes called *personal guilt*, a result of commit-ting sin. This is generally a healthy form of guilt so long as the feelings of guilt have an objective reality. When a Christian commits sin, their conscience is usually pricked because it's informed by God's Word and values consistent with the teachings of Scripture. This guilt affects the emotions and causes sorrow that hopefully leads to repentance.

David sinned by committing adultery with Bathsheba and sending Uriah, her husband, to death. But what did it take for him to realize his guilt? God sent Nathan the prophet to bring the objective real-ity of his guilt home. So when faced with the object reality of his sin, he felt sorry and guilty because in God's sight he was guilty. Psalm 51 records the expression of his feelings and his remorse for his sin. Through confession, his guilt was removed. It is the same for believers today (1 John 1:9).

Servicemembers who have experienced guilt associated with self-blame or survivor's guilt must gain a new perspective on their guilt before they can get beyond its detrimental effects.

Our Conscience and Guilt

The Bible declares we are all guilty before God (Rom. 3:10, 23). Our conscience is God's means of telling us that we are guilty of sin, that we are violators of God's law and his holiness (Rom. 2:14–15).[13] A conscience is a good thing because it shines the light of God's truth on our inadequacies.

Humanity deals with the pangs of guilt in various ways. Some people pursue pleasure; some try to numb themselves by alcohol or drug use. Some engage in a flurry of religious activity or eagerly perform good deeds as a way of dealing with feelings of guilt.[14] According to Hebrews 10, Christ's sacrifice is the only means we have to receive a clear conscience and absolution from our guilt.

Sometimes servicemembers experience shame and guilt for what they fail to do—guilt by omission. Guilt and shame work together to cause emotional and spiritual damage. One of my Soldiers witnessed the suicide of a fellow Soldier in the combat zone, which triggered combat experiences he had from a previous war. He blamed himself because he hadn't seen it coming. He felt that he might have prevented it if he had just been more observant. Maybe he could have taken his comrade's weapon away? He not only blamed himself for the suicide, he also felt ashamed because he didn't prevent it.

There are a lot of servicemembers who suffer like this. They suffer with shame and guilt because of what they failed to do or because of what they perceive to be a failure. No one will ever know if this Soldier could have prevented the suicide of his friend. Hindsight is always much clearer.

Guilt and shame are significant issues for most veterans. The various forms of guilt and shame all have generally the same effect—they lead to dysfunction and ongoing pain. The answer to both of these issues is confession and forgiveness. We'll consider God's answer to guilt and shame in the next chapter. Before we get there, let's look at the biblical concept of shame and how shame is connected to PTS.

THE BIBLICAL CONCEPT OF SHAME

The biblical concept of shame is a subjective response to an objective reality. It is a negative emotion that reflects a wrong action and the presence of guilt. One writer defines shame as "a painful emotion of misery, reproach, and embarrassment, arising from guilt for sin, an unworthy act, or impropriety."[15] He later adds, "Shame is the appropriate evidence of conviction touching anything wrong in God's sight; a reaction against sin, which God himself gives."[16] Its

115

presence indicates conviction and guilt, and may assist the person in confronting wrongdoing, if indeed one is genuinely guilty.

SHAME IN THE GARDEN

The concept of shame is first observed in the Garden of Eden. The Bible declares, "And they were both naked, the man and his wife, and were not ashamed" (Gen. 2:25). Later we read, "But the LORD God called to the man and said to him, 'Where are you?' And he said, 'I heard the sound of you in the garden, and I was afraid, because I was naked, and I hid myself'" (Gen. 3:9–10).

What changed? Sin entered the human race. The inference from these texts is that Adam and Eve were now ashamed. Their nakedness, once innocent and indicative of two people who were rightly related to God, was now an outward expression of an inward problem—guilt. They were guilty before God. Not only did they try to conceal their nakedness, more significantly, they attempted to hide from God.

Shame contributes to alienation from God and from one another. Fear and withdrawal are also indicators of shame. In the story of Adam and Eve, it is important to note the problem of shame is ultimately related to an act of disobedience, a wrongdoing.[17]

SHAME INDICATES GUILT

We may infer from the aforementioned passage that shame functions as an indicator of guilt, attended by withdrawal, fear and alienation as a result of disobedience. Shame is like our conscience, telling us that something is wrong. But our conscience can lie to us when it becomes calloused to the truth (Zeph. 3:5). So long as the conscience is guided by a moral standard, it serves a useful purpose. Shame functions in the same way. It is dependent upon a standard of truth. We feel shame to the extent that a standard has been violated. This is clearly the situation in Adam's case. But we can become insensitive to feelings of shame.

For example, when Absalom conspired against King David, David was forced to flee Jerusalem. Then Absalom, in the sight of all Israel, took David's concubines and made them his own (2 Sam. 16:20–23). He had no shame for the disgrace he brought upon his father or the kingdom by this act of insolence. The standard had no bearing on his actions, and so there was no indication of shame. Jeremiah 3:1–3 also speaks to the lack of shame among those in Israel who, despite their disobedience and God's judgment, refused to repent. We may infer from Absalom's actions and from the nation of Israel that shamelessness may be accompanied by arrogance.

SHAME AND OTHERS

Shame may result from the actions of others. People experience shame from hurts not necessarily due to their own fault. A woman who was raped may feel deeply ashamed because of what happened to her. She may feel embarrassed and accept undeserved blame. But the rape is not her fault. This is a type of false shame that often flows from a sense of false guilt.

Servicemembers may experience this by feeling shame for actions they did not do. This is how the Soldier who could not prevent his friend's suicide felt. But did he deserve the shame? Was the suicide his fault? Did he deserve to feel guilty? Certainly there are other factors to consider in his case. Were there any warning signs? Were there any risk factors present? Given what we know, he didn't see it coming, and thus he probably assumed undeserved guilt and shame and blamed himself unnecessarily for the death of his friend.

Proverbs 19:26 states, "He who does violence to his father and chases away his mother is a son who brings shame and reproach."

While shame and reproach may be borne by the father and mother, it is not due to their wrongdoing but to their son's actions.

Shame and PTSD

The dehumanizing effects of war are well documented in many personal accounts. Such dehumanization, cultivated by desensitization to killing, only contributes to the veteran's grief, guilt, and sense of shame later.

Dehumanization is pervasive and attacks our humanness like a cancer. It can taint the deepest recesses of the soul. The carnage of war muddles the soul's appreciation for grace and beauty, and it may distort one's ability to perceive God's grace, love, and mercy.[18] Many veterans are hammered by shame and guilt or held captive by war's dehumanizing spell; it's a bewitching that leads many to moral ruin.[19]

Shame is often more pronounced in veterans who suffer with PTSD. In a study on shame and its contribution to PTSD, hospitalized veterans diagnosed with PTSD were administered several assessment instruments measuring shame, depression, and self-esteem. Their scores were compared to another group of hospitalized veterans with depression and substance abuse. The results showed that veterans suffering with PTSD scored higher on their internalization of shame and depression than those without PTSD.[20]

I met with a Soldier who served in combat and was being treated for PTSD. He manifested low self-esteem and feelings of shame. When I asked him to tell me what contributed to his feelings, he told me that during the war he had mistakenly engaged friendly positions with his weapon. Moments later, he realized his mistake and ceased fire, but his comrades ridiculed him relentlessly for his mistake. No one was hurt. Given the chaos of war, this type of incident is not uncommon. Yet he felt bad about it and struggled, blaming himself for what he had done. Many months later, he still suffered from shame for that event.

The sense of shame is not something easily erased. It is an intensely painful experience that often leaves the sufferer isolated, diminished, and disconnected from others. This is usually the case because shame is closely connected to self-esteem. People who view themselves this way feel powerless and even trapped.[21] Feelings of desperation and hopelessness emerge, coinciding with fear, confusion, and anger or frustration. Where people find the most support is in the company of others who share similar experiences.[22]

SHAME'S REMEDY

John Newton, a former slave trader who became a Christian and a minister of the gospel, suffered from the lingering effects of guilt and shame. He penned the words to the famous hymn "Amazing Grace," but still wondered how God could save a "wretch like me." He wrote, "I once was lost but now I'm found; was blind but now I see." On his tombstone it reads:

> John Newton, Clerk, once an infidel and libertine, a servant of slaves in Africa, was, by the rich mercy of our Lord and Saviour Jesus Christ, preserved, restored, pardoned, and appointed to preach the faith he had long labored to destroy.

The story of Newton is a story of triumph over guilt and shame. But only through the forgiveness of Christ did John Newton ever experience freedom from guilt and removal of his shame.

Shame like the feeling of genuine guilt, is only remedied by forgiveness and spiritual cleansing. The psalmist prayed, "Cleanse me with a hyssop and I shall be clean" (Ps. 51:7). For those who endure shame and suffer the penalty of guilt, Christ is the answer. Christ is uniquely qualified to solve our dilemma because he bore our shame and guilt on the cross. Moreover, according to the Scriptures, he endured undeserved shame, mockery, and embarrassment on our behalf. He suffered all manner of insults, contempt, and humiliation so that we would not need to. He is the acceptable guilt offering for sin and the bearer of shame (Isa. 50:6–7, 53:1–12; Matt. 27:30).

NOTES

1. Chappelle, "An Air Force Psychologist's."
2. Collins, *Christian Counseling*.
3. Schiraldi, *The Post-Traumatic Stress*.
4. Ibid.
5. A. J. F. Dulley, "Guilt," in *Baker's Dictionary of Christian Ethics*, ed. Carl F. H. Henry (Grand Rapids, MI: Baker Book House, 1981), 279–280.
6. Collins, *Christian Counseling*.
7. Law of war pertains to the legal justification for war and the laws governing conduct in war and after the cessation of hostilities. It relates to just war theory, which is the moral doctrine of war that consists of three ethical components: (1) *jus ad bellum*, ethical rules that apply to the decision to make war; (2) *jus in bellum*, the ethical rules that apply to actions taken in war; and (3) *jus pos bellum*, the ethical rules that apply to the actions ending a war.
8. J. Dwight Pentecost, *Man's Problems God's Answers* (Chicago: Moody Press, 1974).
9. Ibid.
10. Matsakis, Post-traumatic; Decker, "Including Spirituality."
11. Lyles et al., "Trauma and PTSD"; Matsakis, Post-traumatic.
12. Matsakis, *Back From the Front*.
13. Pentecost, *Man's Problems*.
14. Ibid.
15. R. F. Gribble, "Shame," in *Baker's Dictionary of Theology*, eds. Everett Harrison, Geoffrey Bromiley, and Carl F.H. Henry (Grand Rapids: MI: Baker Book House, 1960), 483–484. See also R. L. Cobb, "Understanding the Biblical Concept of Shame," *News for Christians* (2006), accessed February 12, 2013, http://11.newsforchristians.com/sermons037.html.
16. Gribble, "Shame," 483.
17. B. A. Mullen, "Shame," in *Baker's Evangelical Dictionary of Biblical Theology*, ed. W. A. Elwell (Grand Rapids, MI: Baker Book House, 1996).
18. Gray, The Warriors; Tick, *War and the Soul*; Shay, *Achilles in Vietnam*; Grossman, *On Combat*.
19. Tick, *War and the Soul*.
20. M. R. Wong and D. Cook, *Shame and Its Contribution to PTSD*, accessed February 12, 2013, http://onlinelibrary.wiley.com/DOI: 10.1002/jts.2490050405/abstract.
21. Brown, "Shame Resilience Theory."
22. Ibid.

CHAPTER 6

CONFESSION AND FORGIVENESS

*If we confess our sins, he is faithful and just to forgive us
our sins and to cleanse us from all unrighteousness.*

—1 John 1:9

*Forgiveness is essential in life for us to grow and to be
gifts of love: sometimes we need God's forgiveness,
sometimes we need to forgive others, sometimes we
need to forgive ourselves.*

—Fr. Eugene Kole

O N February 3, 1998, Karla Faye Tucker was put to death by the
State of Texas, at that time the first woman to be executed
in America in fifteen years. She was a confessed pickaxe murderer;
but in prison her life dramatically changed through a genuine religious conversion experience. This former drug-crazed prostitute
and savage killer became what many saw as a fully rehabilitated
and beautiful, loving person. Her story demonstrates how even the
worst of us can be changed through Christ.[1]

There is another part of her story that is lesser known. It is the story about the brother of one of Tucker's victims, Deborah. His story is about his struggle with hatred, faith, and ultimately his ability to forgive. Deborah's brother learned to forgive Karla Faye for the brutal murder of his sister. This act of forgiveness did not change anything about the outcome of Karla Faye Tucker. And it certainly didn't bring his sister back. But it changed him and brought healing that otherwise he would never have experienced.

This chapter is about the journey to forgiveness that is necessary for warriors who are suffering from the effects of wartime guilt and shame. For most, the person they find hardest to forgive is not some ax-murderer but themselves.

Guilt is an unnecessary burden for warfighters to bear. God provides a way out of guilt through confession. Servicemembers may find forgiveness through confession of guilt and sin. Christ bore all penalty of sin, including penalties for war atrocities and lapses in judgment. This chapter focuses on the meaning of confession and forgiveness. Practitioners will learn how to lead warriors to discover the benefits of confession and forgiveness available to them through the sacrifice of Christ. These warriors can find redemption from their sins.

THE MEANING OF CONFESSION

Through confession, one acknowledges guilt before God. The act of confession results in cleansing from sin, guilt, and shame. The biblical concept of confession conveys the idea of agreement, promise, or admission.[2] Both Leviticus 5:5 and 1 John 1:9 speak of confessing sin or admitting before God a wrong that was committed. The word translated "confess" in 1 John 1:9 is the Greek word *homologeo*, which comes from two words, *homos*, "same," and *lego*, "to speak." Hence, confession to God involves saying the same thing about one's sin that God says about one's sin.[3]

A person confesses sin when they agree with God, openly admitting guilt and freely declaring the sin by persuasion of the facts and deeply felt conviction (Ps. 51; 32:5; Acts 24:14; Heb. 11:13; Matt. 7:23; John 9:22).[4] When confession of sin is made, a person acknowledges God's law was broken (Ps. 119:126) and God's holiness was violated (Lev. 19:2; Matt. 5:48).

Confession may be expressed as an act of worship. A person may confess that God is sovereign (1 Chr. 29:10–13) or that he is faithful, kind, and loving (Ps. 118:2–4) or that he is the source of help in time of trouble (Ps. 46; 105:1–6).[5] Many of the psalms are expressions of heartfelt confession and adoration, reflecting on the one hand admission of guilt and shame, but on the other, thanks and praise for deliverance and forgiveness of sin (Pss. 22, 30, 32, 34, 40, 51, 116).[6] The Hebrew word translated "confession" can mean both "praise" and "admission of sin," depending upon the context. Both meanings were part of a single concept.[7]

The act of confession is expressed similarly in the New Testament. Confession includes the admission of sin as well as the declaration of praise or allegiance (Matt. 10:32; Rom. 10:9, 10; 1 Tim. 6:12).

CONFESSION AND PTS

Confession is an important concept for addressing the spiritual injuries of PTS. Research indicates victims of PTS deeply desire freedom from real or perceived guilt.[8] "Making a confession" or "coming clean" with God about one's guilt is the means for addressing wartime violations or victim blame. It serves as the portal to forgiveness and reconciliation with God as well as others.

Scripture is replete with examples of those who confessed their sins to God or to a priest representing the people to God, and who confessed the people's sins to God. Job, Moses, Samuel, David, Ezra, Nehemiah, and Daniel are just a few examples. We all bear the burden of guilt for our sins. Through confession, we enter into a right relationship with God, enjoying the benefits of forgiveness.

In Psalm 51, David records his confession of sin and guilt before God. The confession refers to the sin of adultery that he committed with Bathsheba and to the sin of murder that he committed against Uriah, her husband (2 Sam. 11:1–12:25). It is one of the most eloquent expressions of remorse and contrition in the Bible, considering it provides insight into the nature of confession and how it leads to restoration.

Psalm 51: A Prayer of Confession

The 51st Psalm is one of seven penitential psalms in the Bible. The others are Psalms 6, 32, 38, 102, 130, and 143. In this psalm, David exposes his soul and pleads for spiritual renewal and full restoration with God. The Scriptures reveal the importance of renewal and restoration. Warriors in particular, suffering with guilt and shame, deeply desire to be restored and renewed, to return to normalcy and full health. Confession accomplishes this for the guilt-ridden sufferer.

As we consider this psalm, we note David's plea for restoration in verses 1–2. It's a plea for mercy and cleansing according to the extent of God's love. He asks God to act favorably according to his grace, and without punishment because of his mercy (Exod. 34:6–7). David is aware that he doesn't deserve favorable consideration, but he asks anyway because he understands the merciful character of God.

David refers to his sins as "transgressions" and "iniquity" and pleads for them to be blotted out—to be spiritually washed away.

The Old Testament sacrifices and ritual washings symbolized the removal of sin and renewal of fellowship with the Lord. The sacrifices by themselves could not secure salvation or cleansing, but God is free to be gracious to whomever he wants.

In verses 3–6, David acknowledges his deep awareness of sin and offers no excuses, recognizing the severe nature of his offense before God: "Against you, you only, have I sinned and done what is evil in your sight." He is quite conscious of his sin and it's constantly before him. He can't escape reminders of it and its emotional and physical effects. Sin is taking a toll on his spiritual and physical well-being.

His plea is reminiscent of the Prodigal Son, who recognized the nature of his offense, the futility of his life, and its effects on his relationship with his father (Luke 15:18). David, like the Prodigal Son, is content to place his case before God, the Father of Heaven, knowing that God observes his contrite heart. David is confident that God will act justly. He also understands what God requires—inward truth and wisdom. Earlier, this is what David had failed to do—act truthfully and wisely. But now he has quit playing around.

What does God desire? He desires the internalization of his truth. God's truth is external to the heart. It is an objective and absolute reality that exists apart from us. It's an objective standard. Only when we respond to the objective nature of truth on the outside are we changed on the inside. Lifesaving medicine cannot help someone until it's taken. Like medicine, truth must be internalized in order to make us well. This is what David is looking for.

In verses 7–12, David offers his prayer for restoration. The prayer for restoration consists of (1) a plea for God's forgiveness (vv. 7, 9), (2) a plea for renewal of joy (v. 8), and (3) a plea for a heart of wisdom and full restoration to divine favor (vv. 10–12). In verses 7 and 9, David uses the same words he used in verses 1 and 2. He pleads for purging or cleansing and the blotting out of his sins. He prays that the Lord, like a priest, may cleanse him from his defilement. Lepers presented themselves before a priest on the occasion of their purification. The priest, being satisfied that the unclean person had met the requirements for purification, would take a bunch of hyssop, dip it in water, and sprinkle the leper with water, declaring the leper clean. David prays that God will cleanse his heart, dipping the spiritual hyssop in the pure water of God's grace and declaring him clean, too.

With forgiveness and cleansing comes newness of life. Spiritually laundered, David anticipates his cleanliness like a garment freshly washed, "whiter than snow," and relishes the moment he knows again the joy and physical benefits of being rightly related to God, possessing a new heart of truth and wisdom (v. 8). He recognizes that renewal begins with the Lord, who alone can blot out sin, the guilt of sin, and any reminder of it. Such renewal leads to radical transformation, a brand-new heart and a right spirit within him (v. 10).

This state of restoration builds on his newfound wisdom and includes a clean or renewed heart. He once again enjoys communion with God and the presence of God. All of this leads to a deep desire to be used by God in leading others to godly living and corporate worship. It likewise gives the assurance of knowing that God indeed is the God who cleanses and restores (v. 17).

THE MEANING OF FORGIVENESS

On May 11, 2002, a drunk driver killed two women, Meagan and Lisa, devastating their families and friends. But the story of this accident is also a story of forgiveness and healing. Both Meagan's and Lisa's family chose to forgive the twenty-four-year-old drunk driver, Eric.

CONFESSION AND FORGIVENESS

They even appealed to the court to have his twenty-two-year prison sentence reduced to eleven years.[9]

This story later became the basis for Matthew West's song, "Forgiveness." We cannot ignore the spiritual significance and power of forgiveness. The stories of Deborah's brother, who forgave Karla Faye, and of Meagan and Lisa and their families, who forgave Eric, illustrate the power of forgiveness and what it can do to bring healing to people.

Forgiveness is especially relevant to veterans returning from war. As we have learned, many things happen in war that can only be resolved through forgiveness.

We may be able to forgive others for little things they might say or do. But many of us put a limit on forgiveness. How many times do we forgive a spouse for abuse? How many times do we forgive a husband for unfaithfulness? How many times do we forgive a killer or a rapist? The disciples also wondered about this. Peter asked, "Lord, how often will my brother sin against me, and I forgive him? As many as seven times?" Jesus said to him, "I do not say to you seven times, but seventy times seven" (Matt. 18:21–22). According to Jesus, there is no limit to forgiveness.

We've all been hurt by someone's words or actions at one time or another. Such offenses may have been deliberate or unintentional, but either way they still sting and leave us angry or bitter. What is forgiveness? Forgiveness is a deliberate and decisive act of letting go of resentment toward another or of any thoughts of revenge against someone else.[10] It involves a pardon that aims at restoring a broken relationship. To actually restore a relationship requires genuine repentance on the part of the perpetrator, restitution for any losses, and, most importantly, rebuilding trust with the victim, which takes time. While restoration is the aim of forgiveness, it does not happen often. But restoration is not required to forgive.

The idea of forgiveness is a Christian doctrine based on the full expression of God's love as demonstrated in the redemptive work of Christ.[11] Forgiveness is essential to Christian living and reflects the values of grace, mercy, love, and compassion (Eph. 4:32). It is a moral act and a voluntary decision intended to move the relationship beyond trauma to healing and hope.[12]

BENEFITS OF FORGIVENESS

The expression of forgiveness is beneficial. For the offender, it often leads to restoration and peace. And for the offended party, the act of forgiveness not only leads to peace and joy but to better health too. It results in an overall reduction of stress, an increased sense of well-being, lower blood pressure, happier disposition and outlook, and less inclination toward depression.[13] Feelings of resentment, bitterness, or anger no longer have any control over the offended person.

In instances where a person is unable to forgive, there is a significant negative effect. The individual becomes trapped by their own emotions and is unable to move forward with life. Refusal to forgive gives the offender control over the offended.

Some people are so bound by guilt that they find it impossible to forgive themselves or seek forgiveness from God. Unfortunately, lack of forgiveness deeply affects relationships and causes sufferers to be so wrapped up in the past that they cannot enjoy life in the present. This is precisely the problem with many veterans; they are stuck in the past and doomed in the present. Forgiveness sets someone like that free from the past to enjoy the present.

Granting forgiveness does not excuse the other person's actions or deny responsibility for an offense. Eric was still responsible for the deaths of Meagan and Lisa. Forgiving him did not change any of the facts, minimize the injustice, or remove his debt to society. But forgiving Eric contributed to the emotional healing of all parties concerned.

How does someone take the first step to forgiveness? First, recognize the tremendous value of forgiveness. David understood the value of forgiveness and pursued it, even when he didn't think he deserved it. God's compassion and forgiveness is offered freely to anyone who desires it. "Come, everyone who thirsts, come to the waters; and he who has no money, come, buy and eat!" (Isa. 55:1).

Second, the person in need of forgiveness has to consider life without forgiveness, how the lack of forgiveness is affecting her or his life and ruining it.

Third, the person must choose to forgive, whether that choice means forgiveness for oneself or forgiveness of others. It is a deliberate act, resulting in cleansing and freedom. It means the sin no longer has any control over the sinner; it means the offender no longer has any control over the offended. The offense no longer defines the life of the offended.

OTHER EXPRESSIONS OF FORGIVENESS IN THE SCRIPTURE

Various expressions of forgiveness are found in the Old Testament. Forgiveness is based on the character of God and is dispensed to those who are genuinely repentant. Several Hebrew terms and images are used in the Old Testament to describe the idea of forgiveness. The image of the scapegoat conveys the sense that the sins of Israel were "sent away" into the wilderness, never to be seen again (Lev. 4:20; Ps. 86:5; 103:3).

The Scriptures further define forgiveness as an exchange, our sin for God's cleansing (Ps. 32:1–5). In Psalm 32, David uses the same three words he used in Psalm 51 to describe his sin. And then he adds three more words to show the comprehensive nature of forgiveness, essentially canceling the power of sin.[14] First, he uses the word "forgiven," which in its verbal form means to "lift up or take away" (vv. 1, 5).[15] In forgiveness, God removes our sin "as far as the east is from the west" (Ps. 103:12). He takes it away. He wipes it out. This is the image of the scapegoat, bearing the sin of the people and driven from the camp.

Second, David says that his sin is "covered" (Ps. 32:1). The word means "to hide, to clothe like a garment covers one's nakedness." God covers our sin; and he buries it deep so it will never be found, never revealed again.

A third word David uses to describe the nature of forgiveness is found in the expression, "Blessed is the man against whom the LORD counts no iniquity" (Ps. 32:2).[16] God no longer counts our sin against us. The charges are dropped and our account is cleared. This idea is elaborated in the New Testament, where Paul describes forgiveness as a cancellation of debt (Col. 2:13, 14; Rom. 4:5–8).

As an act of divine pardon, forgiveness corresponds with confession. In confession, sin and guilt are freely admitted; in forgiveness, the judgment and penalty of sin and guilt are removed. In forgiveness, God reconciles humanity to himself (Eph. 2:14–17), and humanity enjoys the peace of God (Col. 3:15).

In the New Testament, the concept of forgiveness is amplified in Christ. Christ's death is viewed as the basis for forgiveness (Matt. 26:28). Christ is the only one who has the power to forgive sin (Mark 2:5, 7, 10; Col. 1:13–14). Sin has made humanity indebted to God, but through Christ the debt of sin is removed (Matt. 18:23–35). The idea of sin as a debt is conveyed by the Greek word *aphiemi*, denoting cancellation of a debt, a covering, or a dismissal (Matt. 6:12).[17]

WARTIME STORIES OF FORGIVENESS

There are stories of forgiveness that come out of war. One of the most compelling is the story of Ernest Gordon, a POW imprisoned by the Japanese during World War II. (I mentioned him earlier in chapter 4 in connection to loss of meaning he and his fellow prisoners experienced as POWs.) Their plight was pitiful. Indeed, more than eighty thousand POWs died from beatings, disease, and starvation in just over a year of building the railroad that became known as the "Railroad of Death."[18]

But Gordon, amazingly, survived his imprisonment and was released from the camp at the end of the war and eventually became the dean of the chapel at Princeton University. He had become a Christian as a result of his wartime ordeal, and in the spirit of Christ, he sought reconciliation with his captors and, in meetings after the war, offered forgiveness.

A similar story, popularized by the book and motion picture *Unbroken: A World War II Story of Survival, Resilience, and Redemption*, is the story of Louis Zamperini, a 1936 Olympian and World War II POW.[19] His story is an equally amazing tale of endurance, resilience, and forgiveness. Tortured endlessly by his Japanese captors, he survived the war and returned home, suffering from the effects of PTS.

Resorting to alcohol to numb his pain, he struggled to save his marriage and ended up at a Billy Graham Crusade, where he made a profession of faith in Christ. Reminded of the promise he made to serve God if he survived being cast adrift at sea, he relented at the crusade and gave his life to Christ. Confronted with the teachings of Christ, he decided to return to Japan, seek out his captors, and offer his forgiveness. This act of forgiveness set him free from the most detrimental effects of PTS, and it led him in continued service to Christ.

THE USE OF FORGIVENESS AS A THERAPEUTIC TOOL

Researchers have examined the use of forgiveness as a therapeutic tool to enable victims to transform the wounds of trauma.[20] The majority of research indicates forgiveness is very important and even a critical element for personal healing.[21] Learning to forgive reduces stress, diffuses anger, removes anxiety, and builds confidence and hope.[22]

When people, particularly veterans who've been mistreated or tortured, grant forgiveness to their enemies, new opportunities emerge.[23] The stories of Gordon and Zamperini are just two examples among many others in which people who've decided to forgive their enemies learn to finally put an end to the constant, intrusive cycle of trauma that holds them captive to their symptoms, especially issues with anger, grief, and revenge.[24]

Feelings of entrapment, anger, and hate and desires for revenge are all normal emotions experienced by veterans or by anyone who has been offended or mistreated. For the veteran, deeply traumatized by acts of war, their decision to forgive their enemy begins by facing the reality of the trauma and recognizing its debilitating effects. They come to understand that withholding forgiveness is not worth the cost. They realize that failing to forgive grants more power to the perpetrator. But even contemplating forgiveness requires conditions in which the victim feels safe and has gained some sense of control. Below, we'll look at how forgiveness works.

THE PROCESS OF FORGIVENESS

Forgiveness is a personal choice that is done for the benefit of the sufferer. It's a personal act that requires abandoning resentment and one's right to judgment. It is nurtured by the exercise of compassion and unconditional love.[25]

Choosing to forgive is to enter into a process of spiritual development that promises a movement beyond the traumatic event. Forgiveness ignores neither the severity of the experience nor the guilt of the perpetrator. This was certainly the case for the brother of Deborah and for the families of Meagan and Lisa. Awareness of the wrong that was committed, acknowledgment of the pain that was experienced, and differentiation between the event and the perpetrator facilitate the forgiveness process.

The most important step in the forgiveness process is the decision to forgive. It requires a cognitive change. This process is not immediate but involves complex rethinking of anger, resentment, bitterness, and blame.

Some have suggested the process of forgiveness is more akin to a process of discovery and realization than to a decisive act.[26] Regardless, when a victim, especially one who is suffering from PTS, chooses to forgive, that person discovers the decision to forgive is an empowering choice that restores control to the victim and gives new perspective on the experience.

THE ACT OF FORGIVENESS

The act of forgiveness never excuses the crime or minimizes the offense. It breaks the victim's sense of isolation and victimization, and creates new patterns of interaction. It offers the potential for change and the chance to start over.

Those who choose to forgive, despite painful experiences, enjoy unimaginable healing and peace in the end.[27]. Scarlett Lewis lost her son, Jesse, a first grader at the Sandy Hook Elementary School in Newtown, Connecticut, in 2012. The following year, she published a personal account of the Sandy Hook massacre, expressing her reasons why she thought she could forgive the boy who killed her son and hoping that something good might come from such an awful tragedy.[28]

According to Frederic Luskin, director of the research-based Stanford Forgiveness Project and author of the book *Forgive for Good*, choosing to forgive in instances of tragic loss such as Scarlett's is a natural step toward recovery and healing. It takes the pain away.[29]

NOTES

1. Linda Strom, *Karla Faye Tucker: Set Free* (Colorado Springs, CO: Water Brook Press, 2006).

2. W. A. Elwell, "Confession," in *Baker Encyclopedia of the Bible* vol. 1, ed. Walter A. Elwell (Grand Rapids, MI: 1988), 505.

3. W. E. Vine, "Confess, Confession" in *An Expository Dictionary of New Testament Words* (Old Tappan, NJ: Fleming H. Revell Co., 1966).

4. Ibid.

5. Elwell, "Confession."

6. Ibid.

7. Ibid., 505.

8. Tick, *War and the Soul*; Dewey, *War and Redemption*.

9. See http://matthewwest.com/the-stories/the-story-forgiveness/, accessed December 23, 2015.

10. Mayo Clinic Staff, "Forgiveness: Letting Go of Grudges and Bitterness," accessed March 1, 2014 http://www.mayoclinic.com/health/forgiveness/MH00131; see also J. M. Houston, "Forgiveness," in *Baker Encyclopedia of the Bible* vol. 1, 810–812.

11. Finch, "Trauma and Forgiveness."

12. Ibid.

13. Mayo Clinic Staff, "Forgiveness." See also Julie Exline and Roy Baumeister, "Expressing Forgiveness and Repentance: Benefits and Barriers" in *Forgiveness Theory, Research, and Practice*, eds. Michael McCullough, Kenneth Pargament, and Carl Thoresen (New York: Guilford Press, 2000), 133–155.

14. Eric Geiger, Michael Kelley, and Philip Nation, *Transformational Discipleship* (Nashville, TN: B&H Publishing Group, 2012). On pages 75–79, the authors provide a concise and understandable meaning of these words.

15. F. Brown, S. Driver, and C. Briggs, "*Nasa*" in *The Brown-Driver-Briggs Hebrew and English Lexicon* (Peabody, MA: Hendrickson, 1997), 669–671.

16. F. Brown, S. Driver, and C. Briggs, "*Chashab*" in *The Brown-Driver-Briggs Hebrew and English Lexicon* (Peabody, MA: Hendrickson, 1997), 363.

17. W. E. Vine, "*Forgive, Forgave, Forgiveness*," in *An Expository Dictionary of New Testament Words* (Old Tappan, NJ: Fleming H. Revell Co., 1966) 122–123.

18. As cited in David Stout, *New York Times* (January 20, 2002), accessed June 3, 2013, http://www.nytimes.com/2002/01/20/nyregion/no-headline-223891.html.

19. Laura Hillenbrand, *Unbroken: A World War II Story of Survival, Resilience, and Redemption* (New York: Random House, 2010).

20. Martin Marty, "The Ethos of Christian Forgiveness," in *Dimensions of Forgiveness: Psychological Research and Theological Perspectives*, ed. E. Worthington (Radnor, PA: Templeton Foundation Press, 1998), 9–28; M. McCullough, J. Exline, and R. Baumeister, "An Annotated Bibliography of Research on Forgiveness and Related Concepts" in *Dimensions of Forgiveness*; R. Enright and R. Fitzgibbons, *Helping Clients Forgive: An Empirical Guide for*

Resolving Anger and Restoring Hope (Washington, DC: APA, 2000); Terri-Ann Legaree, Jean Turner, and Susan Lollis, "Forgiveness and Therapy: A Critical Review of Conceptualizations, Practices, and Values Found in the Literature," *Journal of Marital and Family Therapy* 33, no. 2 (2007): 192–213.

21.   Legaree et al., "Forgiveness and Therapy."

22.   Ibid.

23.   Finch, "Trauma and Forgiveness."

24.   Ibid.

25.   As cited in Finch, "Trauma and Forgiveness."

26.   Legaree et al., "Forgiveness and Therapy."

27.   Finch, "Trauma and Forgiveness," 30. See B. Greenfield, "Parents Forgive Driver Two Weeks After She Killed Their Daughters," November 5, 2013, accessed November 10, 2014, https://shine.yahoo.com/parenting/parents-forgive-driver-two-weeks-after-she-killed-their-daughters-201733075.html.

28.   Greenfield, "Parents Forgive."

29.   Ibid.; Fred Luskin, *Forgive for Good: A Proven Prescription of Health and Happiness* (New York: Harper San Francisco, 2002).

CHAPTER 7

DEVELOPING A THEOLOGY OF SUFFERING

Why is this happening to me? What did I do wrong? Why am I going through this in my life?

—An OEF veteran

For I consider that the sufferings of this present time are not worth comparing with the glory that is to be revealed to us.

—The Apostle Paul

TRAUMA often leads to many questions and concerns about suffering. This is an issue for many veterans, particularly with those who've witnessed the senseless loss of life in combat or grieve over the loss of friends or wonder about the meaning and utility of war.

Suffering is complicated and people suffer for many reasons—reasons that often remain obscure. Failure to find meaning for suffering usually contributes to more pain. It's also painful when one tries to reconcile their suffering or the suffering of others with perceptions or beliefs about a "good, powerful, and loving God."

In this chapter, we'll consider the problem of suffering in order to help us understand how many veterans view suffering or struggle with reconciling their combat experiences with their understanding or expectations of God.

Suffering is Universal

Tragedies happen every day. Human suffering is universal. People wonder why? Why this tragedy? Why so much suffering? It was no different in Jesus' day. In Luke 13:1–2 we read this account:

> There were some present at that very time who told him about the Galileans whose blood Pilate had mingled with their sacrifices. And he answered them, 'Do you think that these Galileans were worse sinners than all the other Galileans, because they suffered in this way? No, I tell you; but unless you repent, you will all likewise perish. Or those eighteen on whom the tower of Siloam fell and killed them: do you think that they were worse offenders than all the others who lived in Jerusalem? No, I tell you; but unless you repent, you will all likewise perish.'

Apparently, during the Jewish Passover feast, while certain Galileans were making their yearly sacrifices, Pilate had them killed. We don't know much about this incident; no extra-biblical historical record exists to provide details. In Jesus' day, another event also occurred that led to questions. During what might have been the construction of an aqueduct near the pool of Siloam, a tower collapsed and fell on eighteen construction workers. All of them perished.

People are always looking for reasons for tragedies. It's natural to our humanity. We want to know why bad things happen to people?

Sometimes the reasons are obvious; but many times the reasons are obscure. It would appear that neither the Galilean massacre nor the collapse of the tower had any clear cause. The Galileans were just worshipping God. The construction crew was just doing their job. They were ordinary people, no different from other Galileans or people who lived in Jerusalem.

So it is with tragedies; we do not usually know the reasons for them, and many tragedies appear senseless to us. We can only deal with the effects. So it is with war. War is full of tragedies, trauma, and suffering. These things contribute to other problems and evoke questions much like those posed to Jesus.

When we look at this text in Luke 13 more closely, we notice that Jesus doesn't answer their questions directly. "Do you think that these Galileans were worse sinners than all the other Galileans, because they suffered in this way?" he asks (v. 2). He speaks to their assumptions: "bad things happen to bad people; good things happen to good people." But that's not always the case; and it's certainly not the case in this story. They were innocent—the Galilean worshippers and the eighteen people. It's not easy to reconcile the deaths of innocent and ordinary people particularly when we're left in the dark about causation or motivation. According to Jesus, they were no different than anybody else; and unless we repent, we'll all perish as sure as they did. What does he mean by that? To really understand what Jesus is getting at we need to consider the entire context of Luke 13. This is what I think he's telling us: Learn from these events. Life is unpredictable; and sometimes bad things happen to innocent and ordinary people. He goes on to explain with an illustration of an unproductive fig tree (13:6–9). The landowner wants it cut down. But the gardener pleads with the landowner, "Give it another year. Maybe with a little cultivation, it will produce some figs?" The unproductive fig tree represents the unproductive life—a life lived for self. The landowner is God, the Father, who is about to render judgment on the tree. But Jesus, the gardener, pleads with the Father to allow the unproductive tree—that is, the unproductive person—a little more time to make his life count.

The reason for suffering is not as important as how we respond to it or what we do with our lives because of it. Jesus is telling us to live our lives appropriately and make them count, to make them count for eternity. He's saying, don't ask *Why?* Rather, ask *How? What?* or *What should I do?*

It doesn't matter so much how someone dies but how someone chooses to live.

Numerous Theological Challenges

The incidence of PTS among veterans returning from war presents numerous theological challenges. Combat-induced trauma creates spiritual dissonance and suffering, leading to personal and social dysfunctions. Questions about the morality of war or its justification and the political, religious, and social values of warfighters have bearing on the development of PTS. The effects of PTS touch the deepest places of the soul, often shattering concepts of what is right or good or true. As we've discovered, grief consumes many victims of PTS along with guilt and shame. Servicemembers returning from combat long for reconciliation of their grief, forgiveness for their sin, and cleansing from their shame.

God does not often explain the reasons for trauma, but he does provide the means to get beyond its debilitating effects. Christ's death provides a template for understanding trauma and suffering, along with lessons learned from the stories of Job, David, and Paul, which we'll consider later. Various psalms and New Testament passages contribute to our understanding of suffering and provide principles, which promote understanding, healing, and growth. In due course, we'll look at some of these as well.

In the sections below, we'll explore relevant theological concepts about suffering that may help us understand issues pertinent to the development of PTS and for the treatment of its symptoms.

THE PROBLEM OF EVIL AND SUFFERING

The trauma that produces PTS invariably leads to questions about the source of evil and the problem of suffering. The existence of evil and suffering has always been a major obstacle to faith in God. The problem of evil and suffering is often framed as a question like this: *If God is so good, loving, and all-powerful then why is there such evil and suffering in the world? If God desires to prevent evil but is not able, then he's obviously not all-powerful. If God is able, but not willing, then he's obviously not loving or good. If he's both willing and able, but refuses to act, then he must be totally evil and we should not trust him.* The problem of suffering and evil is the apparent conflict that exists between one's understanding of the nature of God (namely, his power, love, and goodness), as taught in the Bible, and the occurrence of violence and suffering in the world.

The sci-fi motion picture thriller *I am Legend* introduces us to Dr. Robert Neville, a brilliant scientist and seemingly the last human living on earth. He has made it his purpose to contain what is apparently an unstoppable man-made virus that has killed millions and left many others inhuman, mutant victims.

For three years, Neville faithfully sends out daily radio messages, desperate to find any other survivors who might be out there. He continues to work on a cure. But the mutants are watching him and waiting for a moment when he is vulnerable so they can kill him.

Then when he meets a survivor, his despair temporarily lifts. Maybe there's some hope? The survivor, hopeful of a cure as well, brings up the existence of God in a conversation with Neville. But Neville immediately protests, "How can God do anything?" Frustrated and angered, he reasons God is irrelevant. Far too many people have died. It doesn't appear God really cares or is very capable; otherwise, he would have done something about the spread of the virus, Neville rationalizes.

Many veterans who are victims of PTS struggle with the problem of evil and the suffering of the innocent. Like Dr. Robert Neville, they question God's actions or perceived lack of action. *If God is real and powerful as he says he is, why does he permit so many to die such terrible deaths? Why does he allow so much evil in the world?* or *Why did he allow my friend to die?* The problem of suffering, the veteran's inability to reconcile what he has experienced with what may have been learned in church or at home contributes to much pain and spiritual trauma.

The story of Job is a powerful and compelling example of suffering in Scripture. It provides insight into how one may cope with suffering, and offers some explanation about the source of evil. We learn from Job that while God permits evil, he is never the agent of it. We discover that while God allows for suffering, he does not usually explain it. (Recall Jesus' reply in Luke 13.)

Scripture teaches God is good, loving, and all-powerful. But he's also righteous, just, and holy. He's sovereign in the exercise of his authority over the affairs of humankind, and has created a world that allows for the existence of both good and evil.[1] Since he is sovereign and just, he seeks justice and righteousness in all that he does, receiving glory that only he deserves. He never justifies his actions nor typically explains his reasons for what he does.[2] Frankly, he's not accountable to anyone or anything. Yet people ask,

"How can such a God continue to allow so much evil, injustice, and suffering?" It's their inability to reconcile this dilemma satisfactorily that often leads to a personal crisis of faith—and for some, to an interminable impasse.

But God calls each of us to faith, to trust him and in him no matter the circumstances that we may find ourselves in. He invites us to accept his provision for salvation in the Person and work of Christ who died for our sin, who was buried, and who physically rose again from the dead on the third day. He wants us to enjoy the blessings of forgiveness and the gift of new life. But nowhere does he exempt us from pain or evil. While Jesus prayed for us that we might be kept from the "evil one" (John 17:15), he never promises a troubled-free life. What he did promise was that we'd have peace in him. "I have said these things to you, that in me you may have peace. In the world you will have tribulation. But take heart; I have overcome the world" (John 16:33).

God's people have always wondered about the presence of evil or their suffering. We've asked God, *Why?* or *When?* or *How long before…?*(Ps. 6:3; 13:1; 73; Hab. 1:2–3). We live in a world of evil or random acts of evil that defy rational inquiry. The prophet Habakkuk wondered why it seemed God wasn't listening, why so much violence persisted, or why God even tolerates it?

Peter predicted suffering and pain for Christians who would stand for the faith and the testimony of Christ (1 Pet. 3:13–17). Joseph suffered unjustly, being sold into Egypt and imprisoned for nearly thirteen years. He may have despaired of ever being rescued. Yet, in God's time Joseph was vindicated and was able to report: "As for you, [his brothers] you meant evil against me, but God meant it for good, to bring it about that many people should be kept alive, as they are today" (Gen. 50:20). God gives meaning to suffering. What is meant for evil may also be meant for good. In Joseph's situation, the very act of evil resulted in a greater good and the preservation of many lives.

Evil exists in the world because of sin (Gen. 3; Rom. 8). Evil represents the rejection of God and the corruption of all that is good. It is derived from Satan and the sin that exists in the human heart (Job 1–2; Jer. 17:9). Christians are affected by evil because they live in an evil world (John 16:33); they are also affected by evil because they are not without sin (1 John 1:7–9).

God apparently uses evil for his own purposes. He has purposed to draw us to himself so that we might look to him, so that we might completely trust him (See Ps. 37). The Apostle Paul once pleaded with God to end his suffering and remove his "thorn in the flesh" (2 Cor. 12:7–8). But God refused. Job, a righteous and just man, suffered immeasurably and persistently, losing his health, his wealth, and his family. God not only refused to end his suffering, he deliberately allowed it. In these instances, God fulfilled his purposes; he revealed himself in ways that would not have otherwise been known. Paul discovered God's grace is sufficient and his power is made perfect in weakness: "For the sake of Christ, then, I am content with weaknesses, insults, hardships, persecutions, and calamities. For when I am weak, then I am strong" (2 Cor. 12:10).

God has seen fit to include evil in his plan. But nothing goes on without his permission. That seems clear from the story of Job. But God never takes responsibility for the evil that occurs.[3] God stands behind evil in such a way that the evil transacted never infringes on his holiness or is charged to his account. Similarly, as we see from Peter's account in the book of Acts, chapter 2, verse 23, though God delivered up Jesus according to his plan, it was others who were held accountable for Jesus' death. Consider what we would not have known or experienced if Jesus Christ had not died for sin?

He was innocent. He did not deserve to die at the hands of evil men. Yet Christ's death fulfilled a greater plan for humanity. Consider also Job's outcome or Paul's?

The question posed by the problem of evil and suffering is inadequate because it perceives God in a limited way. It takes certain attributes of God and creates a "this-means-that" equation. God is more than "loving, good, and powerful." Much more. God reveals himself in many other ways as we have observed above. He created a world that calls for faith; that includes multiple "equations" demanding multiple responses. Such responses always include faith but also reveal greater knowledge of God that otherwise would not have been known except by the experience of suffering and evil. If there were no evil acts or painful sufferings, we would never know heroes, we would never know of extraordinary love or selfless sacrifice.

Some people have trouble accepting these things because their faith is small; and their understanding of God is very limited. Small faith vanishes at the first sign of suffering; but great faith remains firm and grows because of suffering. People think of evil and suffering in a closed system that doesn't allow for a loving and powerful God who would permit the existence of evil. We need to think about God differently. It is mostly true that through the window of pain we look to God and see him differently. God cares more about that than what we think he should do.

Believers should take heart from the promises of God that while they may suffer and even die prematurely, God is present and deeply cares (Isa. 41:10). He walks with us through our fiery ordeals. He gives all believers his Holy Spirit, who serves as their Guide, Comforter, and Companion for life's journey (John 14–16).

Knowing that he walks with us enables us to go through deep waters confidently and courageously. While he does not always deliver us out of every trouble, his purposes are perfect and his will is accomplished. He always remains with us and never abandons us (Heb. 13:5b–6). And, as the poet reminds us, when it sometimes seems he is no longer walking beside us, it is then that he is carrying us.[4] Or as the psalmist tells us, "He leads me beside still waters. He restores my soul. He leads me in the paths of righteousness for his name's sake. Even though I walk through the valley of the shadow of death, I will fear no evil, for you are with me; your rod and your staff, they comfort me" (Ps. 23:2b–4).

While we cannot explain all suffering and evil, Scripture teaches that ultimately suffering is due to the presence of sin. People commit sin and suffer the effects of their choices. God dealt with sin through the cross of Jesus Christ. God continues to graciously offer salvation to all, patiently waiting, and delaying final judgment so that more people might repent and choose Christ (2 Pet. 3:9).

All creation groans from the effects of a fallen world (Rom. 8:18–15). We suffer from disasters; all the things humans have no control over. But one day God will right all the wrongs and create a new heaven and a new earth in which all suffering will cease, death will be no more, and righteousness dwells (2 Pet. 3:13; Rev. 21:4). There's a better future for creation and all believers. We can understand that future when we place our present suffering in its proper light. As Paul reminds the Corinthians: "So we do not lose heart. Though our outer self is wasting away, our inner self is being renewed day by day. For this light momentary affliction is preparing for us an eternal weight of glory beyond all comparison, as we look not to the things that are seen but to the things that are unseen. For the things that are seen are transient, but the things that are unseen are eternal" (2 Cor. 4:16–18). There's a greater purpose for our suffering. This eternal purpose causes all temporal pain to pale in significance.

And one day the world will be set free from the effects of its bondage and decay; one day all suffering will cease and death will be no more (Rom. 8:18–25; Rev. 21:4).

THE PURPOSE OF SUFFERING

In the book *The Five People You Meet in Heaven*, the author tells the story of Eddie, who, on his eighty-third birthday, dies while saving a girl who has been in an accident at the amusement park where he works. Eddie is a maintenance worker at the Ruby Pier amusement park and apparently has worked as the park's maintenance worker for many years since returning from the Pacific War. When he awakens in the afterlife, he encounters five people with ties to his former earthly existence. They help him understand the meaning of his life and its value. Each person he meets shares with him a valuable life-lesson, which helps him gain a new perspective on his seemingly tragic and insignificant existence.

One of the people he meets in the afterlife is a former member of his military unit who was killed in the war. As this encounter plays out, Eddie suddenly finds himself standing on a battlefield. The smoke of expended artillery rounds along with the stench of burning flesh tells him that many Soldiers died there including the Soldier who accompanies him. It's obvious to Eddie that the suffering and loss were great. It all appears so tragic and senseless. But Eddie is about to learn some valuable lessons.

This is really the issue when it comes to suffering. Things do not make sense. We are limited by our humanity. We are limited by our temporality. We lack eternal perspective. We find it difficult to see what is unseen, to perceive what is eternal. We're trying to figure everything out, but we do not possess the insight, wisdom, or experience to explain it all. In short, we're not God.

God is weaving the tapestry of our lives. We sometimes can't make sense of it, but that's just our perspective. We're looking at it from the underside, but he sees it from the upper side. To him, it all makes perfect sense. But there's coming a day when we'll understand the threads he used and why they were woven in. But until that day, we must trust his judgment in the things he weaves into our lives.[5]

Perhaps this is what Paul is trying to tell us in Romans 8:28 when he says, "And we know that for those who love God all things work together for good." Compare this statement to Genesis 50:20. Sounds similar. The fact is we do *not* know; we are instructed here to take it by faith. We must trust God. He is the "Master Synergist". He's working it all together for his glory and for his purposes. It's not fate that makes things so. God's fingerprints are on all of it. Yet he acts without incurring any blame to himself, for if he deserved blame, he would not be God.

So what does Eddie learn? He learns from his former commander everybody loses in war. Some lose their limbs, some lose their lives, and all lose their innocence. Still others lose their sense of purpose or their perspective. They return from war with visible and invisible wounds, and they find it difficult to get their lives back on track. That was Eddie. Eddie, wounded and scarred, thought he'd lost every-thing in war. But that is the nature of war. It's sacrifice. It's costly. But he learns that sacrifice is also a noble thing. It is the thing that makes us human.

Giving of oneself for the benefit of others or for larger ideals is also redemptive. It means something. It counts. It has value. So loss and suffering must be understood differently. They must be viewed from a different perspective. Eddie learns in war "all give some and some give all"—their lives, their futures—"their last full measure of devo-tion." But Eddie let his loss make him bitter and angry. He failed to learn the lesson of sacrifice. Now, at the time of his death, he finally learns the lesson. His sacrifice mattered too. His life mattered. His life made a difference.

Many veterans today are just like Eddie. They have a problem with suffering because they have not learned the lesson of sacrifice. They have not discovered the purpose of their suffering.

THE SUFFERING OF CHRIST

Having an understanding of Christ's suffering provides another means to comprehend our own suffering, particularly as it pertains to the nature of sacrifice and God's purposes behind suffering. The suffering of Christ fulfilled God's purposes. His suffering was an undeserved suffering. He was completely innocent. Peter writes, "He committed no sin, neither was deceit found in his mouth" (1 Pet. 2:22). Yet, as we read further, it is by his suffering that we receive healing (1 Pet. 2:24b): "By his wounds you have been healed."

According to Isaiah, the suffering of Christ was necessary in order to bring healing to humanity. It served God's purposes (Isa. 53). Scripture teaches the sacrifice Christ made was for our good. It accomplished the forgiveness of our sin (1 Pet. 2:24; Col. 1:13–14). His sacrifice satisfied the righteous demands of God, who requires payment for sin (1 John 2:2). Through Christ's suffering, God dealt with evil and enabled healing, forgiveness, and reconciliation for humankind (2 Cor. 5).

According to the writer of Hebrews, Christ was uniquely qualified to become our Savior. His sacrifice uniquely achieved God's purposes, the very purposes that Christ was destined to fulfill. This is what the writer means when he says, "For it was fitting that he, for whom and by whom all things exist, in bringing many sons to glory, should make the founder of their salvation perfect through suffering"

(Heb. 2:10). God's plan and purposes for redemption were completed or perfected through the suffering of Jesus.

Did God kill the Son? No. He is never the agent or source of evil. Yet God accomplished redemption for humankind through evil means and evil men who perpetrated a capital crime against the innocent Christ (Acts 2:23–24). It was in God's plan and fore-knowledge; yet, men did the deed. By this masterful synergy, God achieved his purpose and revealed in Jesus' death incomprehensible meaning and nobility. His sacrifice mattered; it made a difference, a big difference.

USING CHRIST'S SUFFERING TO UNDERSTAND OUR OWN

Through the death of Christ, including all his suffering throughout his life, we learn about our own suffering (Heb. 5:7–9). We discover the meaning of our suffering. His passion moves us beyond the problem of evil and sin. It teaches us about the meaning of sacrifice and the purpose of service. It opens our imagination to the possibilities that come with a life that serves ideals larger than self. This is why there is value in sacrifices made for others or why even in war there are noble and redemptive actions.

Suffering opens the door of the soul to reflection and inquiry. We must contemplate Christ's death in the context of his life, his teachings on discipleship, his ministry of compassion, and his relationship with God, the Father. In this respect, we may look at our sufferings differently, asking the questions, "Is there some meaning that we can derive from our experience that might contribute to our spiritual growth or create a deeper sense of commitment?"[6] "Is there something in our suffering that might lead us to a closer walk with God?"[7] Or, "Can such serious reflection on suffering, particular Christ's suffering, connect us to him more intimately, resulting in a deepening of our relationship with him and leading us in our own suffering to renewal and healing?"[8] Maybe you might think about these things the next time you receive Communion.

Indeed, all suffering should teach us how to live and make us better people. It should facilitate the development of the soul, enrich our being, and make us whole persons. Is this not what Peter is saying? "But rejoice [in your sufferings] insofar as you share Christ's sufferings, that you may also rejoice and be glad when his glory is revealed" (1 Pet. 4:13). Could it be there is great benefit in sharing in Christ's sufferings? Peter seems to think so. This is apparently how God wants us to view suffering. He wants us to understand that we are connected by our sufferings to Christ's sufferings. Moreover, we should aspire to share in his sufferings as something that deepens our commitment to Christ (Phil. 3:10).

SUFFERING AND THE BREVITY OF LIFE

Suffering instructs us in the importance and brevity of our lives. It stimulates us to live godly and productive lives. Tragic losses and the suffering of those associated with those losses are not intended to motivate us to explore the rationale behind their occurrences. Rather, they occur to remind us that life is short. Our end is unknown but certain. We can use tragic events to learn how to live better, God-honoring lives.

Life is short and unpredictable. Our life is a vapor, a morning dew, here for a little while and then gone. We need to make our lives count. The psalmist summarized it this way: "So teach us to count our days that we may get a heart of wisdom" (Ps. 90:12).

Recall the unproductive fig tree in Luke 13. A life that is lived with selfish purpose is a life that is always taking but never giving back. Like the fig tree that drew its nutrients from the ground and lapped

up the rain but never produced any fruit, some people live unproductive lives, unfamiliar with sacrifice. They never make any contribution. But Jesus is patient with them. He works with them so that
their lives might count for something.

SUFFERING AND OUR CALLING

Suffering may help us identify our calling in life. Nick Vujicic was
born without limbs.[9] When he was eight, he contemplated suicide;
and at the age of ten, he tried to kill himself. What kind of life does
someone have who has no arms or legs?

But Nick found a special calling and purpose for his life. While he
is not able to do conventional things that people with arms and legs
do, he has found unconventional ways of doing things. He speaks
to young people all over the world about his special situation, and
how God has blessed him despite his disabilities.

He tells young people that they do not have to look to drugs, alcohol, or premarital sex for meaning. It's Christ who gives fulfillment to
life. So many young people resort to suicide because of despair and
lingering depression. But through his losses, Nick has been used by
God to lift young people from their despair to hope, acceptance, and
meaning in their lives. Nick found purpose in his suffering because
he came to understand the meaning of it.

SUFFERING AS OUR COMMON BOND WITH HUMANITY

While suffering often isolates the victim, we may look at our suffering as the common bond of our humanity and solidarity with others.
When we sense this communalization of suffering, we gain conso-
lation and derive a sense of communion and connectedness with
others. This is what Paul means when he says we enter into the
"fellowship of Christ's suffering" (Rom. 8:17; Phil. 3:10; 2 Cor. 1).

We share in Christ's suffering as a community. We share with one another. That bond strengthens us.

THE TRANSFORMATIVE POWER OF SUFFERING

Do not underestimate the transformative power of suffering. For Christ, who was motivated by great love, his passionate suffering turned into spiritual triumph—enlarging possibilities not only for him but also for the rest of us. Thus, the crucifixion of Christ did not thwart the benevolent purposes of God but rather fulfilled them. His death fulfilled God's purposes on several levels: it dealt with sin and evil, enabled humanity to accept suffering and its purposes, and gave meaning to human life. An evil enacted became the instrument of healing and life. The resurrection event demonstrates this reality. What humankind meant for evil, God meant for good.

So God allows evil to achieve his purposes. The traumatized followers of Jesus did not understand God's purposes on Good Friday, but later, on Resurrection Sunday, they began to understand. The death of Jesus was initially incomprehensible for the disciples, but gradually they learned to see things differently (Luke 24:20b, 21a; Matt. 16:22).[10] Traumatized by the death of Jesus, their assumptive world was in disarray. The trauma of Jesus did not make any sense. How could the Redeemer of Israel die? How could he establish his kingdom if he was dead? When they began to revise their thoughts and adapt to new ways of seeing things (reframing the narrative of the trauma), they were able to think differently, feel differently, act differently, and thereby gain a renewed sense of hope. This is how a traumatic event produces growth and leads to healing. In truth, no one could have imagined the outcome of Jesus' death.

The world in which we live is a world of suffering, pain, and injustices (Job 5:7). While God does not often intervene to change this suffering, he has intervened through the cross of Christ to bring about a world without suffering. But it is a world not yet in evidence. People must learn that this world of suffering is the first of two worlds. The second world promises healing, hope, and freedom from suffering (Rev. 21:4).

Ways to Explore Suffering with Those Who Suffer

How caregivers explore this subject with the sufferer is important to the healing process. While God may use trauma for many reasons, some known and others unknown, the caregiver should be cautious about identifying the reasons for the sufferer. We understand from Scripture that sometimes suffering is a consequence of sin (2 Sam. 12). Often it is used to test faith (Job; Jas. 1:2–4; Rom. 5:3–4; 1 Pet. 1:6–9) or provide some spiritual lesson on suffering (John 9:2–3; 1 Cor. 10:6; 2 Cor. 12; Heb. 12:3–11). But many times none of these reasons apply. For example, in Job's case, none of the explanations he received from his counselors accounted for his suffering. It is better to guide the sufferer through the array of possible reasons for trauma than to decide for him.

It is even more helpful when the pastoral counselor points the sufferer away from the question of *Why?* to the question of *What?* or *How? What does God want you to do with the suffering you're experiencing?* Or ask, *How will you respond to what happened?* Or *How can you find meaning in this?* Avoid telling people they're suffering as a result of sin even if it appears obvious to you. Let them discover this for themselves. While we condemn sin and warn people of God's judgment (the prophet Nathan comes to mind), it is an entirely different matter to tell someone their particular suffering is the result of sin or their lack of faith. I doubt we can always know that. But God can reveal it to them. He has many ways to do that. I remember the time my wife lost her sister to cancer. It was a very painful loss. She was young and left behind four little children. Someone told my wife at the time that her sister would not have died if my wife had more faith. Really?

God does not necessarily use suffering as a tool of punishment (John 9; Luke 13). In the case of Christians, it is important to remember that Christ bore the punishment of sin, though he was sinless. It is more likely God uses suffering to develop faith, to instill confidence in God, and to deepen dependency on him. If God is giving a lesson on faith or discipline, then I believe God will reveal this to the person (2 Cor. 11; Heb. 12:3–11; 1 Pet. 3:17, 4:12–19).

We may never know the reasons behind our suffering. Dogmatic assertions about God's reasons for suffering or trauma are usually not helpful. The clergy's role is to facilitate understanding and guide the sufferer through self-discovery. Not to do this is to deny a victim the opportunity to process his or her own suffering. It may also lead to false blame or open old wounds.[11]

Sin and evil entered this world through Adam's disobedience and at the instigation of Satan (Gen. 3:1–7; Rom. 5:12). The presence of sin has brought about great suffering and pain (Gen. 3:14–19). Sin has tainted all of creation; all of the natural and moral evil that exists is the result of sin's entrance into the human race (Gen. 3; Rom. 8:20–22).[12]

God has responded to the presence of evil and suffering through redemption. One day the accomplishments of the cross of Christ will end the curse of sin and death (Rom. 5:15–21; 1 Cor. 15:20–28; Rev. 22:3). One day the Scripture will be fulfilled: "He will wipe away every tear from their eyes, and death shall be no more, neither shall there be mourning nor crying nor pain anymore, for the former things have passed away" (Rev. 21:4).

Pastoral caregivers must come to their own understanding of suffering. It must be an understanding that enables them to address the issue of suffering with people who are in deep pain from the effects of PTS, as well as with others who may be suffering for other reasons. It all begins with understanding the nature of God—not just his power, his love, or his knowledge—but all his attributes. Only then might we come to understand the presence of evil and the reasons for human suffering. Remember Christ. His suffering serves as a paradigm for understanding all suffering as well as a means for acquiring healing.

NOTES

1. Morton Smith, "Theodicy," in *Baker's Dictionary of Theology*, 517–518. See also John 9:2–3 and Isaiah 45:7.
2. Carl Laney, *God* (Nashville, TN: Word Publishing, 1999).
3. Ibid.
4. See http://www.freewebs.com/footprintsiamauthoranonymous/whowrotefootprints.htm.
5. See http://tapestrychurch.com/life-is-but-the-weaving-the-tapestry-poem-corrie-tem-boom/
6. Liza Rankow, "The Transformation of Suffering," *Pastoral Psychology* 55, no. 1 (2006): 95.
7. Ibid.
8. Ibid.
9. See http://www.lifewithoutlimbs.org/.
10. Joanna Collicutt McGrath, "Post-traumatic Growth and the Origins of Early Christianity," *Mental Health, Religion & Culture* 9, no. 3 (2006): 291-306.
11. Fuller-Rogers, *Pastoral Care*.
12. Laney, *God*.

CHAPTER 8

THE TRAUMA NARRATIVE

But when I thought how to understand this, it seemed to me a wearisome task, until I went into the sanctuary of God; then I discerned their end.

—Asaph

THE experience of trauma is irreversible. We cannot change what happened to someone who was traumatized. But we can help that person change the way she or he views the experience. Life is like a script, composed of events and choices—some good, some bad—enacted by a cast of characters. The story line is supposed to make sense. But trauma dramatically affects the script. It totally disrupts the storyline.

Sufferers struggle to make sense of their traumatic experience. How do we make sense of death and violence, the loss of comrades, or the loss of innocent civilians? How do we comprehend the suffering of the innocent and the magnitude of war? How do we fit the experience of trauma into the script?

So far we've examined the spiritual effects of trauma, particularly the many forms of loss associated with trauma, reasons for suffering, the seemingly inexplicable nature of evil, and concepts of confession and forgiveness associated with guilt and shame. In this chapter and in the remaining chapters, I explain the concepts of narrative reconstruction and narrative reframing. The use of narration when addressing traumatic experiences is an effective technique for correcting cognitive distortions associated with trauma.

I'll apply these concepts to the suffering of Christ and other biblical models for healing, which teach new ways of viewing trauma and aid in healing. We'll learn through the passion of Christ (building on what we discovered in chapter 7) and through the experiences of Job, David, and Paul how trauma has an "upper side" unseen by us. While we may understand more as we acquire new information and insight, we also recognize that sometimes we understand less. However, the example of Christ and the experiences of Job, David, and Paul all illustrate how trauma may be reframed to provide new meaning and enable healing for the traumatized who come into your care.

The Trauma Narrative

Learning to reconstruct the trauma narrative and reframe trauma in religious terms leads to healing, post-traumatic growth, and greater satisfaction for many victims. These two aspects of narration are extremely useful in learning to reappraise events using biblical stories.[1]

Generally, the use of stories helps by enabling servicemembers to connect emotions with facts and events. Stories clarify perceptions. When stories are told in the company of others, confidence is built in the sufferer and the expression of support is enabled. We learn from one another's stories and experiences. Talking eases the pain associated with trauma.

Narration may be verbalized or written. Both are useful techniques. When conducted in the context of a supportive, caring group, such as a church group or a group of fellow veterans, the interaction is therapeutic. Also, retelling the story tends to normalize the trauma and reduce the stress associated with it.

NARRATIVE RECONSTRUCTION

Narrative reconstruction is an essential element of debriefing. When used effectively, it addresses not only the facts associated with the traumatic event but also the victim's perceptions that involve thoughts, emotions, and actions. Its use normalizes the traumatic experience. Employed early on, reconstruction mitigates negative stress reactions that typically occur later, such as PTS.

In narrative reconstruction, the warrior is encouraged to relate the traumatic event in orderly detail, to address misconceptions and distortions. Since the experience of trauma is so emotionally laden, memories may be distorted. The retelling of the event serves to clarify perceptions, with the goal of normalizing the traumatic event for the sufferer.

According to some research, the retelling of the traumatic story reduces its power over the sufferer, which serves to normalize the effects of the traumatic event.[2] (While the event itself is extraordinary, the reactions are normal.) Emphasizing the normalcy of PTS reactions counters the negative perception of some that leads them to say, "I have a mental disorder." Though this assessment may be clinically accurate, I don't think it contributes to positive outcomes. I would rather emphasize the sufferer, diagnosed with PTSD, is reacting normally to an extraordinary or abnormal event(s).

Writing about the event is another way of using narrative reconstruction. Writing can help people share more easily their most painful thoughts. Writing identifies the sources of pain and addresses those sources in ways that can lower stress.[3] One variation of "traumatic writing" is artistic expression through drawings or paintings. I've observed its use and believe it is also therapeutic.

NARRATIVE REFRAMING

Narrative reframing incorporates new information into the narrative so that the sufferer may be able to separate the memory of the traumatic event from the painful emotions associated with the event. Narrative reframing is often used with narrative reconstruction, and their goals are the same—to correct distortions and perceptions. In narrative reframing, however, the idea is to incorporate new information so that perspectives are adjusted. The new information changes the script, and the result is the acquisition of a different perspective of the traumatic event.

Reframing trauma, sometimes referred to as *cognitive restructuring*, not only requires the introduction of new information but the willingness of the sufferer to explore new possibilities. The introduction of new information dramatically affects the emotional link to the trauma by reducing the power of the emotions associated with the memory of the event.

Another way of understanding how reframing works is to imagine a box. Let's suppose that within the box, ordinary life experiences occur. Life is lived inside this box. Everything has its place; life is predictable.

Things operate according to accepted standards and expectations. But suddenly and unexpectedly, trauma strikes. It takes the victim outside the box, outside the range of ordinary human experience, creating dissonance, disruption, and potential for dysfunction.

Reframing is enlarging the boundaries of the box in order to contain or accommodate the new experience. It's building a bigger box. Or to use another analogy, it's enlarging one's circle of assumptions.[4]

Narrative reframing works well with cognitive behavioral therapy. It's effective when used with narrative reconstruction and when religious themes are included. Both are evidenced-based treatments that show great promise and are easily adaptable when making spiritual interventions.[5]

REFRAMING CHANGES THE PERSPECTIVE

You can also think of reframing like opening the lens aperture of a camera. Trauma causes a person to "zoom in" on what has happened to them. Victims tend to focus on themselves; they become introspective. In a sense, they experience tunnel vision and lose all of their peripheral vision. They are so close to this experience they cannot see "the forest for the trees." Reframing forces the victim to "zoom out" and adjust the picture. It changes the perspective. Undetected images emerge. More is revealed. A new appraisal constrains the sufferer to adjust preconceived notions, biases, or misconceptions. When we introduce new information, we enlarge the picture, and it requires a bigger frame.

REFRAMING DELINKS THE PAINFUL MEMORY

Reframing the narrative provides a new perspective that helps sufferers discover meaning in their trauma by connecting their present experience to past experience in a way that delinks the painful memory of their trauma from their present experience. If sufferers can account for their traumatic episodes by the introduction of new information, then they are able to assign meaning and find a place for it in their stories. The assignment of meaning to the event moderates emotions. The activity helps the victim place the event back in the past where it belongs, lessening the emotional connections the victim is making in the present. The original event has less power over the victim in the present, which is the goal of treatment—to lessen the intrusion and regain functionality.

Reframing, then, is successful when the constant reliving of the trauma is transformed into simple remembering the trauma. This process gives the wounded warrior perspective on the enduring present, providing the ability to place the trauma in the past. By doing so, the veteran is relieved of enduring the past in the present, and gains an appreciation for the future.[6] This is making peace with memory; it's putting the past where it belongs.[7]

Biblical Models for Healing

Theologically and spiritually speaking, these narrative themes resonate and should enable healing in veterans, who learn again to remember. Biblical models for healing—exemplified in the stories of Job, David, and Paul, along with the paradigm of the cross of Christ—all point to the efficacy of reframing the trauma narrative in ways that lead to healing. I am persuaded that these stories and similar stories, if they strike an emotional chord with the sufferer, can facilitate an emotional disconnect from the traumatic past.

The Benefits of Reframing the Narrative in Religious Terms

Others have successfully accommodated the use of narration and cognitive reframing to religious themes.[8] They have concluded religious reframing of traumatic events is beneficial for those suffering from PTS. In an article on religious reframing in *The International Journal for the Psychology of Religion*, the authors predicted the use of religious themes in writing about emotionally laden events would moderate participants' mood states. Fifteen participants with PTSD wrote about their PTSD-triggering events in three sessions. Eighty percent of the participants included religious themes in their narratives. In those cases where religious themes were evident, a positive mood change was noted by the time of the third writing session, whereas those who did not use religious themes continued to indicate negative moods.[9]

In sessions I conducted, I encouraged journaling so participants could record their reactions and insights from group appraisal activities. Participants shared with the group anything they wanted from their journals. I found that participants who shared their reactions and insights experienced an improvement in their perception of wellness. Like debriefing activities, journaling provided a way for servicemembers to check their feelings, thoughts, and actions.

Reframing goes hand-in-hand with narrative reconstruction. Normalization is evident when the sufferer is able to relate his or her experience without severe emotional reactions. It is not unusual for a person to react to distorted perceptions of trauma. Through narrative reconstruction, the sufferer is able to clarify what occurred. With the aid of a facilitator and in the company of fellow sufferers, the activity is effective.

In a feasibility study I conducted during my research, I used several reframing activities. In one case, I explored the use of a psalm as a tool for assisting warriors in reframing their trauma in positive and healing ways. Each participant was encouraged to identify the particular trauma or event mentioned in the psalm, identify the symptoms expressed by the psalmist about the event, and then discover how the psalmist was able to reframe his experience, given new information revealed in the text. Participants found this exercise profitable. Many psalms may be used in this way. In other exercises, the group considered various passages that were connected with the death of Christ and explored how witnesses to the death responded to new information about the trauma of Christ.

With this information, participants were challenged to make connections to their own trauma and draw lessons from the experiences of the early disciples.[10] In the next chapter, we'll consider an example of narrative reframing that pertains to the crucifixion.

Recasting Assumptions

When we learn to reframe the trauma narrative, we are recasting assumptions about our experience. All of us have assumptions about how the world operates, such as "The good are rewarded and evil people are judged" or "God always keeps us safe." But we also know that things do not always operate according to our assumptions.

The story of Job is a great example. When things occur outside the sphere of our assumptions, they challenge our worldview and create dissonance. This is often how trauma works. It disrupts. It challenges our assumptions and our beliefs. When a trauma victim learns to incorporate biblical or new information into the equation of suffering, they discover new insights.

Recasting the Narrative: Psalm 73

Psalm 73 offers a classic illustration of how narrative reframing works. In the psalm, Asaph, while acknowledging the goodness of God to those who are good, readily admits his inability to comprehend the prosperity of the arrogant and the wicked. "But as for me, my feet had almost stumbled, my steps had nearly slipped. For I was envious of the arrogant when I saw the prosperity of the wicked." He assumed that while God blesses the good, he also curses the bad. But this was apparently not the case. The wicked people he observed flourished. "For they have no pangs until death; their bodies are fat and sleek." Indeed, they are full of pride and readily defy God himself. How can this be? It doesn't make any sense. In the chart below (fig. 8.1), I apply the reframing concept to the situation of Asaph from Psalm 73.

Traumatic Event	His inability to comprehend the prosperity of the arrogant and the wicked.	Ps. 73:2–3
Traumatic Effects	He stumbled. He was envious. His soul became embittered.	Ps. 73:2, 3, 21
Assumptions	God blesses the good and curses the bad.	Ps. 73:3
New Information	What appears to be the case is not true. The wicked will perish and come to a catastrophic end.	Ps. 73:17–20, 27
Reappraisal	God is always with us. He is sufficient. He will guide us and keep us. It is good to be near God and make Him our refuge.	Ps. 73:1, 23–28

Figure 8.1: The Reframing Concept

We've learned that trauma often interferes with our concepts of what is right, true, and good. Typically, a warrior who is suffering from the effects of a traumatic episode—let's say the unexpected loss of a comrade—has many questions or concerns. She may ask, "Why did this happen?" Or she may comment, "This doesn't seem fair!"

He may question, "How did this happen?" Or he may exclaim, "This doesn't make any sense!" These reactions are all valid. They represent the varied and most certainly accurate responses of warriors, men and women, who struggle with a traumatic episode. Let's look at these responses more closely.

Responses to Trauma

- **Why did this happen?**

  This question explores the problem of meaning and the sense of invulnerability that many servicemembers experience. Typically, a younger, less experienced servicemember cannot imagine their own demise. *It can't happen to me!* They find it difficult to accept their vulnerable position. But the reality is quite different. We are all vulnerable to trauma, regardless of whether we are in combat or not. We live in a world in which bad things happen. Good people die early deaths. Children die. People suffer. War devastates millions. Sometimes it seems the ungodly get all the breaks. This was the observation of Asaph. He struggled with this observation. It nearly toppled him. It nearly ruined him.

  The other part to this issue is the question of meaning. As we have observed in other places, warriors wonder why. It's the job of pastors and caregivers to assist warriors in discovering the meaning of their experiences. Sometimes, as in Asaph's case, meaning becomes clear and assumptions are clarified. But in other cases, we may never know the precise meaning of a trauma. Job never received a clear and precise answer for his trauma, but he understood enough, later on. He was able to go on with his life, albeit a radically different life.

- **This isn't fair!**

  This is another response often expressed by warriors who have been through a terrible situation. It is a reaction to apparent injustice. This was also the reaction of Asaph. He found it difficult to reconcile his concept of justice with what he observed among those who disregarded God. He played by the rules. He kept himself pure. But being good did not result in the outcome he expected. "All in vain have I kept my heart clean and washed my hands in innocence," he exclaimed. He didn't get any breaks. "For all the day long I have been stricken and rebuked every morning," he moaned.

  The problem of fairness resides in one's perception. No one knows everything. We are limited, finite, and frail human beings. But many servicemembers continue to suffer from their inability to reconcile what they observe with their concept of justice. Such perceptions lead to other problems like guilt and enduring grief.

- **How did this happen?**

  This question implies a frequent assumption: *This is not supposed to happen.* It reflects a limited perception, a tunneled view of the situation. The answer is simple: It did happen. Reframing or enlarging one's "box" will accommodate the occurrence. The question gets at the problem of making meaning of the event. It goes with *Why did this happen?* As rational creatures, all people desire to make sense of things. This was the case with Job and his friends. They all wanted to make sense of his situation. They needed to.

  This question may be easier to answer than the why question we examined above. When one asks *How?*, the process that led to the outcome is explored. The harder assumption, *This is not supposed to happen*, gets at one's worldview. If one accepts a world that is unfair, violent, and seemingly arbitrary, one is actually more prepared to deal with the question of how. Accepting a sovereign God, who allows evil for his purposes but never accepts responsibility for evil, can accommodate the seeming incongruity.

- **It doesn't make any sense!**
  This observation is a variation of the search for meaning, which is so critical for healing. Through the expansion of perception and the acquisition of new information, a servicemember may discover a pattern to what seemingly doesn't make sense. This was the situation with Asaph. He found sufficient insight in the presence of God to accommodate his observations about the wicked. This is how life works for many of us. If only we can get a glimpse of God and a little peek at his plan, then we may realize God knows it all and will not abandon his people in the end. Many of the psalms serve this purpose.

Indeed, Asaph discovered much about himself, about God, and about his relationship to him. This leads to another observation about trauma: the problem of identity loss. Trauma often brings into question one's view of self. Asaph was not only able to learn how to accommodate his observation of the wicked; he also learned how special he was in the sight of God. Having once thought he was "brutish and ignorant" about the matter, he realized God was there for him, holding him, and guiding him. He concluded, "My flesh and my heart may fail, but God is the strength of my heart and my portion forever." God remained his dwelling place. God gave him a new identity. Asaph successfully reframed the narrative of his experience to accommodate his trauma, which resulted in new realization, new insights, and personal healing.

Pastoral caregivers should work toward a similar epiphany when assisting servicemembers in reframing their trauma narratives. At the moment when a warfighter realizes the meaning God has for them, the servicemember is able to fit the event into their life script. I'm convinced that if a person can work through this process, they will gain understanding and find healing.

NARRATIVE RECONSTRUCTION AND SCRIPTURE

Narrative reframing is critical to the healing process. Narrative reconstruction is also very important. I believe the reconstruction of the trauma narrative is the first step to be taken by the warrior who is struggling with the effects of combat-related trauma. Again, narrative reconstruction is the retelling of the traumatic event to clarify what actually occurred and the role an individual played in the event. It is ideally suited to critical incident stress debriefing, and it's an effective tool if used soon after the event. But it's also useful later, when a servicemember may be suffering from post-trauma stress. It's a tool used with various treatments, such as trauma incident reduction (TIR) or exposure therapy.[11] The idea, similar to reframing, is that with the retelling of the event, the emotional memory associated with the event is normalized or "delinked," and the power of the event over the individual (its intrusiveness) is lessened.

The Exodus story is an example of narrative reconstruction in Scripture. The Israelites endured four hundred years of slavery in Egypt, and their collective experience was traumatic. Their dramatic rescue from Egypt under the leadership of Moses, and the subsequent failure of Israel to enter into the Promised Land immediately, resulting in forty years of wandering in the wilderness, was also traumatic. As we consider this story in the Bible, we note it is often restated in part, to remind the people what happened to them and how God had rescued them. I believe the historical reconstruction of this trauma narrative served to normalize their national experience and contribute to their national identity. The retelling of the story not only reminded the people of their failures but also of God's care and his promises to his people. It reminded them of God's redemptive purposes.

Another example of narrative reconstruction is the periodic restatement of God's covenantal promises. A cursory survey of the Old Testament reveals that God often reiterates his promises to Israel and particularly to those whom he anoints to lead his people. Interestingly, the occasions of these restatements are commemorated in some fashion, usually by the construction of altars and the offering of sacrifices, and occasionally by congregational assemblies.

Consider the covenants. The Abrahamic Covenant is amplified in the Davidic Covenant; the Mosaic Covenant (the Law) is reframed in the New Covenant (Gen. 12; 2 Sam. 7; Exod. 19–20; Jer. 31). These reconstructions serve as reality markers for the people; they are reminders of God's promises. They clarify God's purposes for his people. They guide the people toward their national destiny.

MEMORIALS AND COMMEMORATIONS

Similar conclusions may be drawn from the use of memorials or memorial statements in Scripture. Whether it is the retrieval of twelve stones from the Jordan River for the construction of a memorial or the assembly of the nation to recite the "blessings and the curses," these acts of memorialization commemorate events and contribute to the national memory. Their use secures tragic or triumphant events to the past enabling the people to focus on the future either unencumbered by failures or inspired by victories.

We do the same in modern times. The Alamo Shrine, the *U.S.S. Arizona* Memorial at Pearl Harbor, and the 9/11 memorials all serve to solidify our national narrative. They say, in effect, "This is what happened here." They serve as reminders of the sacrifices that were made and the significance of those sacrifices to the nation. Memorialization enables healing because it assigns meaning to the event. It honors those who made the sacrifices and places emotional distance between the event and those who survived, facilitating the delinking of the memory from the emotions, putting the past where it belongs.

Individually and collectively, we look to these memorials as markers of the past that remind us of actual events. But they are past events, less burdened by the emotions that once accompanied them. That's another goal of story reconstruction—putting the past in the past and moving on with the present and into the future where the events of the past and the emotions associated with them no longer crowd memories.

THE CIRCLE OF ASSUMPTIONS

In the figure on the following page of Robert Hicks' "Circle of Assumptions," the victim is trauma-focused.[12] The circle of assumptions is narrowly focused and does not accommodate the traumatic event(s) represented by the *X*'s. (The *X*'s are outside the circle.) The circle is divided into quadrants, each reflecting a primary concern of the victim. In the upper left quadrant, the concern is invulnerability, the assumption is "the traumatic event can't happen to me," and the effect is fear and confusion, an outcome commonly experienced by victims of trauma.

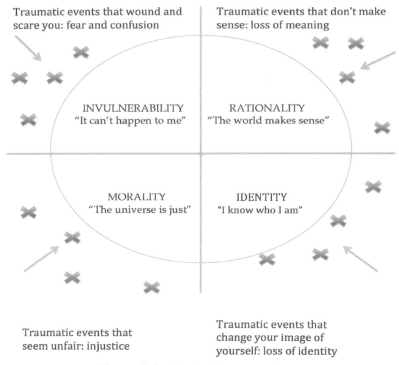

Traumatic events that wound and scare you: fear and confusion

Traumatic events that don't make sense: loss of meaning

INVULNERABILITY
"It can't happen to me"

RATIONALITY
"The world makes sense"

MORALITY
"The universe is just"

IDENTITY
"I know who I am"

Traumatic events that seem unfair: injustice

Traumatic events that change your image of yourself: loss of identity

Figure 8.2: Circle of Assumptions

In the upper right quadrant, the concern is rationality, the assumption is "the world makes sense," and the effect is loss of meaning. In the lower left quadrant, the concern is morality, the assumption is "the universe is just," and the effect is a sense of injustice. In the lower right quadrant, the concern is identity, the assumption is "I know who I am," and the effect is loss of identity.

Victims may experience stress in all quadrants, depending upon the trauma and how it is appraised. Regardless, the victim must learn to enlarge his or her circle of assumptions to accommodate the trauma. Reframing opens the circle to make room for the trauma.

What happens when victims expand their circles of assumptions? They are forced to revise their assumptions to accommodate their experiences. They move from being trauma-focused to being reality-focused. They come to recognize that one can do everything right and still experience tragedy. They learn to accept the things they cannot change. They look for meaning in their pain and hopefully find it. They come to understand the world is a mean place and many things are not fair. But more may be realized.

This is what it means to reframe trauma. It's what Hicks calls "enlarging your circle of assumptions." With new information, there is a new *realization*. The victim comes to understand that God will deal with the inequities of life. God will judge evil men (as in Asaph's situation). God will honor those who are faithful to him despite their suffering. This life is not everything. There is a future and a hope. The story of Joseph is an excellent illustration of how God uses evil and suffering to accomplish his purposes—purposes not immediately apparent to the victim but eventually clarified and realized.

While this does not explain everything, it gives assurance that God is engaged, aware, and in control, though it may not seem so at the time. In the next chapter, we'll observe how the cross of Christ explains how there can be great meaning in suffering which may also lead to profound healing. It explains how God uses the same evil event to accomplish good.

Notes

1. For example, Shay, *Achilles in Vietnam*; Tick, *War and the Soul*; Matsakis, *Post-traumatic*; Herman, *Trauma and Recovery*.
2. S. Bisbey and L. Bisbey, *Brief Therapy*.
3. Julie J. Exline, Joshua M. Smyth, Jeffrey Gregory, Jill Hockemeyer, and Heather Tulloch, "Religious Reframing by Individuals with PTSD When Writing About Traumatic Experiences," *The International Journal for the Psychology of Religion* 15 (2005): 17–33.
4. Hicks, *Returning Home*; Exline et al., "Religious Reframing."
5. Exline et al., "Religious Reframing."
6. Ibid.; Hicks, *Returning Home*.
7. Grossman, *On Combat*.
8. Exline et al., "Religious Reframing."
9. Ibid.
10. McGrath, "Post-traumatic Growth."
11. For more information on TIR see S. Bisbey and L. Bisbey, *Brief Therapy*; for brief discussion of cognitive restructuring see Edward M. Carroll & David W. Foy, "Assessment and Treatment of Combat-Related Post-Traumatic Stress Disorder in a Medical Center Setting," in *Treating PTSD, Cognitive-Behavioral Strategies*, ed. David W. Foy (New York: The Guilford Press, 1992), 39–68.
12. Hicks, *Returning Home*, 150.

CHAPTER 9

THE TRAUMA OF THE CROSS: A NARRATIVE FOR HEALING

The supreme truth of Jesus is that because He went through things Himself He can help others who are going through them.

—William Barclay

I N the 1969 novel *Master and Commander*, there is a seaman who discloses unsettling information to some members of the crew: at one time, he worked as a "sin eater."[1] For this revelation, the crew ostracizes him. The term sin eater refers to someone who, upon the death of a member of the community, would ceremonially take on the sins of the recently departed by the ritual consumption of food and drink provided for him. It was believed that this act absolved the deceased and allowed them to rest in peace.[2]

By some accounts, the ritual was practiced in England and Scotland, and later among the Welsh in America's Appalachia. Usually a beggar performed the ritual as a means of livelihood. Members of the deceased's household would employ the beggar by bringing them to the dying person's bedside, where one of the relatives would place a piece of bread on the chest of the dying person and pass a drink over them to the beggar. A recitation was spoken upon the death of the person. Then the beggar would consume the bread and the drink, symbolizing the deceased member's sin and taking it upon themselves.

The role of the sin eater was popularized in the 2007 motion picture *The Last Sin Eater*, which portrayed a community of Welsh immigrants in Appalachia in the mid 1800s.

In this story, a young girl is convinced she is to blame for the tragic death of her sister, and she is tormented by guilt. In her quest for redemption, she searches out the man in the village who is known as the sin eater. Along the way, she meets an itinerant preacher, who explains to her that the man she seeks has already come, and his name is Jesus. It is not necessary for the sin eater to take away her sin. Jesus Christ has already done so. Through his passion and resurrection, Christ served as our Sin Eater. He paid the price for our sin by taking upon himself its penalty, its shame, and its guilt. He died for us.

The crucifixion of Christ is not only central to the gospel, but functions as a religious narrative and symbol for sufferers of PTS. The cross and the circumstances surrounding the death of Christ help explain suffering and provide a way to discover meaning in suffering. The death of Christ is the means for absolution of all guilt and shame.

Understanding and applying the redemptive work of Christ serves as a healing balm for the soul shattered by trauma. In reality, Christ experienced the greatest trauma, and he empowers his church to be the healing community in which those who face trauma find hope and healing.

The message of the cross, God's provision for sin, is what a sufferer needs. Appropriating the message of Christ leads to cleansing from all forms of guilt, the removal of shame, and the provision for many other benefits, such as a new identity in Christ, new strength through Christ, and lasting hope because of Christ. The gospel enables victims of PTS to experience the presence of God in the depths of extreme suffering. Christ's passion reflects the traumatic experience of war in all of its ugliness, isolation, and injustice.[3] Understanding the meaning and reality of Christ's passion facilitates healing, resilience, and growth. Applying the lessons of the cross brings about all sorts of spiritual healing and affects the individual's entire well-being (Isa. 53).

CALVARY'S CROSS

The redemptive aspects of the cross include understanding the role of the Holy Spirit, his indwelling presence, and his work of regeneration (Rom. 5:3–5; 8:14–17; Titus 3:5–7). Regeneration produces a "new self" which, according to Scripture, "is being renewed in knowledge after the image of its Creator" (Col. 3:10). This regenerative concept speaks to the believer's intrinsic worth before God. It identifies their uniqueness in the new creation as one who has been given a new identity, one who has been transferred from the "domain of darkness" to the "kingdom of his beloved Son" (Col. 1:13).

The believer's new status before God poses new possibilities, imparts new insights, and provides hope for renewal—the very things sufferers desire to receive. A believer's union with Christ qualifies the believer to share in the accomplishments of Christ—his death, burial, and resurrection—resulting in a new kind of life, free from the enslavement of sin (Rom. 6:3–11). Believers are citizens of heaven and are loved and accepted by God (Gal. 2:20; Phil. 3:20; 1 John 3:1). Through spiritual adoption, all believers are treated as sons and enjoy the benefits of sonship, including unfettered access to God and a newfound intimacy with him (Rom. 8:12–17).

An understanding of the cross of Christ leads one to explore the problem of evil and suffering. Through the cross, we address the various and multifaceted dimensions of suffering, including guilt, shame, fear, pain, isolation, abandonment, and loss. The cross reveals the physiological, psychological, and spiritual effects of trauma.

Jesus' crucifixion and subsequent resurrection suggest hope for the sufferer. The traumatic event of Christ's death finds new meaning in the resurrection. On one hand, there is tragedy; on the other, there is triumph. Addressing the juxtaposition of tragedy and triumph, we learn there is great utility in understanding trauma and personal tragedy through the lens of Christ's crucifixion. That event and its consequences suggest personal suffering may also be viewed as something beneficial and an occasion for growth.[4]

This reinterpretation of suffering is an example of reframing the narrative of trauma. Scripture indicates much good can come from trauma and pain (Jas. 1:2–4; Rom. 5:3–5; Gen. 50:21). It provides, for those who embrace it, the enduring sense of Christ's presence in their lives, a perception of sharing in a greater purpose, and the knowledge of the availability of God's resources.[5] The crucifixion event is a story that, understood in its entirety, leads to hope.

In *Psychological Trauma, Christ's Passion, and the African American Faith Tradition*, the authors suggest *theologia crucis* (theology of the cross) fortified the faith of African American Christian slaves.[6] Their expression of faith in Christ effectively enabled them to cope, to endure suffering, and to gain strength from their experience. Slavery, with all of its shameful experiences of rape, beatings, degradation, and brutality, manifested itself in countless instances of dissociation, numbing, and post-traumatic dysfunction. And yet, despite slavery's traumatic effects, many African Americans found the ability to cope by relating to the passion of the Christ. The African American experience was truly a traumatic experience for many black families, extending through generations, and it testifies to the vitality of their faith and life.[7] They showed the rest of us the way by appropriating, symbolically and truly, the meaning of the cross to the problem of trauma and suffering.

In a similar way, the veteran may view a traumatic experience through the lens of Christ's passion and find strength to cope with the effects of trauma. They may discover a new perspective, derived from identifying some meaning from suffering, and actually conclude that suffering is life affirming and not the reason for despair.[8] The veteran has hope in suffering because they have also found meaning in it.

CONCEPTS THAT ENABLED THE AFRICAN AMERICAN SLAVE

For many African American slaves, Christ's passion was not only a motivation for coping; it also moved them beyond their present suffering toward future possibilities. It gave them a positive outlook.

The cross gave African Americans strength in their daily suffering and hope for a better tomorrow. It's possible for sufferers who embrace the gospel to find similar strength through the expression of their own suffering in Christ.[9] This is especially important given the feelings of powerlessness and despair victims of PTS often experience.

Those who suffer from PTS, with all of its spiritual complexities, can learn from the African American experience. They can emulate the African American experience of suffering, finding in it a sense of communalization of trauma—a shared experience that is understood and affirmed. Their stories may also serve as a source of inspiration and unlimited possibilities.

A sufferer can so identify with Christ that they gain a life-changing perspective on their pain just as slaves did. African Americans, though unsettled by unanswered questions about their own suffering, nevertheless looked to God and chose to share their fate with Christ. They identified with Christ in all of the brutality, the injustice, and the senseless violence and despair. They derived from that identification a perspective that enabled them to cope and hope for a better tomorrow. Their existence was reflected in the reality of the cross. That's how they saw it.[10]

Indeed, Christ became sin for all of us so that we might all be rescued from the power of sin over our lives. But African Americans found something more in his suffering and death. They found a paradigm for their own suffering, and their identification with Christ enabled them to endure and overcome.

RENEWED IDENTITY AND NEW LIFE

Some describe PTSD as a loss of identity. The need of the veteran suffering from PTSD is renewed identity and new life. Through Christ, the veteran finds these things. This prospect is possible through Christian conversion, in which one's identity is completely transformed through the death of Christ (Rom. 6:4–11). By union with him in death, his death becomes our death. His accomplishments become our accomplishments. Moreover, by our sharing in his resurrection, his resurrection becomes our entrance into new life (Rom. 6:4–5; Eph. 2:8–9).

This transformation enables spiritual freedom. In the case of the sufferer, it not only gives life but also rehumanizes. The salvation that is received reinstates human value and dignity. The cross of Christ, once viewed as an instrument of shame, is now the means of glory and rebirth (Gal. 6:14). The old self is dead and the new man is born (2 Cor. 5:17).[11] This is precisely what the sufferer needs—a way out of the old life, a way out of the slavery of trauma that continues to remind the sufferer of the past and all the pain associated with it.

God's Entrance into Life's Tragic Dimensions

Philippians 2:1–11 describes the humiliation, death, and triumph of Christ. Jesus Christ "made himself nothing, taking the form of a servant," and "humbled himself by becoming obedient to the point of death, even death on a cross." Christ became one of us and one with us so that we might receive healing and life. Jesus says, "For even the Son of Man came not to be served but to serve, and to give his life as a ransom for many"(Mark 10:45). Christ gave his life so that humanity might live.

The word for ransom in the New Testament Greek is *lutron*, literally "a means of loosing."[12] It signifies for the believer the paying of a price to set a slave free (Matt. 20:28; Lev. 19:20). Christ's death made amends for sin and satisfied God's penalty for sin (1 John 2:2). He died in our place, and his death satisfied the righteous demands of the Father.[13]

In Ephesians 1:7 and Colossians 1:14, Paul uses a similar form of *lutron* to describe forgiveness and justification.[14] Christ redeemed humanity by his death and in doing so provided both freedom from guilt and entrance into eternal life (Rom. 6:4).[15] While it is true Christ died for all of humanity (1 Tim. 2:6; 1 John 2:2), the individual appropriation of Christ's redemption is by the exercise of faith (John 3:16; Rom. 10:9–10; 1 Cor. 15:1–4).

The passion of Christ included many things and various horrible sufferings (Matt. 16:21–23). He was betrayed by one of his own (Matt. 26:47–56). He was wrongly accused, and though completely innocent, was convicted of a capital crime and sentenced to a cruel death (Matt. 27). His closest associates denied and abandoned him (Matt. 26:47–75). He endured mocking and suffered shame (Matt. 27:27–31; Ps. 22:16–18; Heb. 12:2; 1 Pet. 2:21–24). He became accursed (Gal. 3:13–14; cf. Deut. 21:22) and forsaken by God (Matt. 27:46). No words compare to the description Isaiah provides: "He was despised and rejected by men; a man of sorrows, and acquainted with grief; and as one from whom men hide their faces he was despised, and we esteemed him not" (Isa. 53:3).

Pastoral caregivers may refer their clients to these various aspects of trauma in the passion of Christ, for these aspects are the same types of post-trauma effects that warriors experience. They would do well to recognize that in Christ they find a man who has experienced the debilitating effects of trauma, including injustice, shame, and abandonment.

THE MEANING OF CHRIST'S SUFFERING

Christ's suffering was essential for the salvation of humankind. Hebrews 2:9–10 teaches that Christ, by his suffering, qualified himself to be the founder of our salvation. Verse 10 says, "For it was fitting that he, for whom and by whom all things exist, in bringing many sons to glory, should make the founder of their salvation perfect through suffering."

Christ's suffering fitted him for the task of redemption. The word translated "perfect" is *teleioun*, which comes from the adjective *teleios*. According to William Barclay, "The basic meaning of *teleios* in the New Testament is always that the thing or person so described fully carries out the purpose or the plan for which he or it was purposed and designed."[16] Hence, in his suffering, Christ fulfilled the purposes of God regarding the redemption of humanity. Christ's humanity made our redemption possible. Barclay concludes, "If Jesus had come into this world in a form in which He could never have suffered, He would have been quite different from men; He would have been no Saviour for men."[17]

Christ's identity with humanity through suffering enabled him to sympathize with humanity (Heb. 4:15). It is precisely his humanity that enables the sufferer to relate to him and identify with him. As one who is uniquely qualified to save humankind and sympathize with it, Jesus understands human need and provides help (Heb. 4:15–16). Barclay adds, "The supreme truth of Jesus is that because He went through things Himself He can help others who are going through them."[18] Here in this passage is an important point to emphasize as you work with warriors suffering with PTS: Jesus is qualified to help. He shares suffering and pain with all of those who suffer today. He knows what it's like because he has experienced it.

Jesus was God's Suffering Servant, chosen to bring healing and hope for the brokenhearted and spiritually oppressed (Luke 4:18–19; cf. Isa. 61:1–2). His message was liberty (Luke 4:18–19), and he made freedom possible through his own death (Isa. 52:13–53:12; Rom. 3:24; Eph. 1:7; Col. 1:14). Isaiah writes, "He has borne our griefs and carried our sorrows; yet we esteemed him stricken, smitten by God, and afflicted. But he was wounded for our transgressions; he was crushed for our iniquities; upon him was the chastisement that brought us peace, and with his stripes we are healed" (Isa. 53:4–5).

While evil is everywhere and countless suffer, the great theological answer for suffering is found in Christ, who endured unimaginable suffering by addressing a greater plight than evil—the problem of sin. Through his suffering, humanity finds the healing balm of forgiveness, experiences reconciliation with his Creator, and gains eternal hope. One writer observes, "In reconciliation [people] become identified with a suffering God, whereby there is a transmutation of their own sufferings (Rom. 8:15–17 RSV), from pessimism to optimism, from confusion and uncertainty to immortal hope for the banishment of suffering (Rev. 21:4)."[19] The cross is the portal to new life. In the cross, sufferers find meaning and purpose for their lives. It is also God's answer to evil.[20]

In the chart below, I show how the narrative of Christ's suffering may be reframed, resulting in a complete reappraisal of the cross and what it means for the believer. In the same way, a person suffering with PTS may reframe their traumatic experience upon application of biblical information—new information that reframes the narrative of suffering and results in a new perspective that challenges one's original assumptions.

Traumatic Event	The suffering and crucifixion of Christ.	Luke 24:13–35
Traumatic Effects	The disciples lost hope and fell into despair, doubt, and unbelief.	Luke 24:21,25
Assumptions	Christ was the One to redeem Israel. He would set up His Kingdom on the earth.	Luke 24:21
New Information	His body was missing. The writings of the prophets that stated Christ should suffer and enter into his glory. He is alive.	Luke 24:25
Reappraisal	It was necessary for Christ to die in order to redeem Israel and the world. What was a tragedy is actually a triumph.	Luke 24:26–35

Figure 9.1: Reframing the Narrative of the Cross — Luke 24

NOTES

1. Patrick O'Brian, *Master and Commander* (Philadelphia: J.B. Lippincott, 1969).
2. See http://www.deathreference.com/Sh-Sy/Sin-Eater.html; http://www.logoi.com/notes/sin-eaters.html.
3. James A. Noel and Matthew V. Johnson, Sr., "Psychological Trauma, Christ's Passion, and the African American Faith Tradition," *Pastoral Psychology* 53, no. 4 (2005): 361–368.
4. McGrath, "Post-traumatic Growth," 303.
5. Ibid., 291–306.
6. Noel and Johnson, "Psychological Trauma."
7. Ibid.
8. Frankl, *Man's Search*.
9. Noel and Johnson, "Psychological Trauma."
10. Ibid. See also Philippians 2:1–11.
11. Ibid. See also Romans 6:5–11.
12. W. E. Vine, "Ransom," in *An Expository Dictionary of New Testament Words*, 247.
13. Ibid.
14. Everett F. Harrison, "Redeemer, Redemption," in *Baker's Dictionary of Theology*, 438–439.
15. W. E. Vine, "Redeem, Redemption," in *An Expository Dictionary of New Testament Words*, 263–264.
16. William Barclay, *The Letter to the Hebrews* (Philadelphia: The Westminster Press, 1957), 19.
17. Ibid., 20.
18. Ibid., 21.
19. Julian C. McPheeters, "Suffer, Suffering," in *Baker's Dictionary of Theology*, 506.
20. Noel and Johnson, "Psychological Trauma."

CHAPTER 10

BIBLICAL MODELS FOR HEALING

Naked I came from my mother's womb, and naked shall I return. The LORD gave, and the LORD has taken away; blessed be the name of the LORD.

—Job

I N this chapter, we explore the problem of suffering and the effects of trauma in the lives of Job, David, and Paul. While their experiences varied, each of them came to a new understanding about their suffering. They learned things about themselves, about others, and about God that they would not have learned otherwise. Their lives serve as models for healing for others. While God did not often relieve them of pain, their ability to reframe their narratives of suffering enabled them to find meaning in suffering and get beyond the paralyzing effects of trauma.

The Effects of Trauma Observed in the Life of Job

Suffering reduces life to essentials. It has a way of clarifying what really matters. This is certainly evident in the life of Job. The story of Job provides a textbook model of suffering that features the questions often evoked by suffering: *Why is this happening? What did I do to deserve this? Where is God in my suffering? What does this suffering mean?* and *How do I move beyond my suffering?* Gaining an understanding of Job's experience with suffering is very useful in dealing with PTS.[1] It's worth the effort to explore Job's situation, first to help the reader develop a useful view of suffering, and second to help others understand their suffering and find healing.

The Magnitude of Job's Suffering

Job's suffering was undeserved, yet he suffered immeasurably. His trauma was all-encompassing, affecting him physically, emotionally, mentally, and spiritually. His suffering was not a result of sin nor did his suffering induce him to sin (Job 1:22; 2:5, 10). He suffered multiple losses, including the loss of his family, his possessions, his position in the community, and his health.[2] In addition to physical losses, he suffered shame and ridicule. He suffered from loneliness and isolation. He suffered misunderstanding from others, resulting in interpersonal conflict, fear, and confusion. His losses contributed to immense grief—complicated grief, disenfranchised grief, in which nobody seemed to understand his losses. The friends who came to comfort him were baffled by his reactions, and they offered no real or accurate solutions for the problem of his pain.

The Inexplicability of Job's Suffering

Job suffered because he was good. He lived an exemplary life. He was a man of extraordinary faith and spiritual discipline. But God permitted Satan to inflict pain upon Job so that he might demonstrate Job's integrity (Job 1:11–12, 2:9–10). Despite repeated attacks from Satan, Job refrained from sin and refused to give up on God (Job 2:9–10, 13:15). He maintained his integrity despite the increasing severity of his pain and his inability to know its meaning. He resigned himself to his plight, placing his confidence in God and recognizing that God does what he wills and rarely explains himself to anyone.[3] God is sovereign over all; he does what he pleases. Tragedy and blessing are both in the plan of God (Eccl. 7:14). In some ways Job's experience with suffering actually gave him some reasons to endure. While those reasons didn't explain everything or remove the pain, he managed to avoid despair by refusing to renounce his faith in God (Job 13:15).

The Lessons Learned from Job's Suffering

We learn from Job's suffering by observing the new lessons God prepared for him. In those lessons, Job gained knowledge and an experience of God that he discovered through the window of suffering.[4] Whatever Job knew about God personally and theologically was apparently insufficient. Though he was a righteous man and served as a religious leader in his house, God allowed the trauma of suffering to teach him new things about the nature and activity of God (Job 1:1; 1:8; 2:3). Job learned through his suffering about the power of God, and whatever he did not learn from his religious duties and practices, God taught him through his sufferings (Job 42:2).[5] He came to understand the ways of God, that God's purposes cannot be thwarted, that God's power is all-encompassing, and that, while God may be heard, the revelation of God is altogether overwhelming and leaves one speechless. Confronted with these realities, Job could only acknowledge his spiritual poverty and need for repentance (Job 42:1–6).

Through suffering, Job learned new things about himself, his capacity to endure, his commitment to his own integrity, and even his own sense of dignity. He also gained a practical perspective on his suffering. Traumatic experiences turned his theoretical and theological knowledge of God into personal reality. He came to understand how the trauma of life contributed to his life story. In the end, when it seemed he had nothing left, he looked to God and found in him all that he needed.[6]

God was not only sufficient for Job when everyone turned against him; he also vindicated Job and addressed all the injustices Job had experienced. In the end, God defended Job's integrity. His suffering became the means of experiencing a dimension of God and an understanding of himself that he would not have otherwise known. At the end of the story, Job experienced a new level of intimacy with God. He realized the unseen Creator was not only present with him but was present for him. This was perhaps the greatest lesson for Job.

Job never learns the reason for his suffering. God never divulges his unseen plan. What Job does learn is that God does what he wills and that God is powerfully present in our lives. He is always there in our suffering and is quite aware of our pain.

There are lessons here for trauma victims. The innocent suffer, and many others suffer unjustly. Peoples' explanations for this reality are usually insufficient, and the answers to our pain are not often available. But there is always meaning in suffering. God uses suffering to change us and lead us to places of greater knowledge, deeper experiences, and newfound realizations.

In the chart below, I depict Job's trauma. He was able to reappraise his suffering by reframing his trauma narrative in a constructive manner, which led to healing.

Traumatic Events	Loss of family Loss of health Loss of wealth	Loss of status Unjust criticism
Traumatic Effects	Physical pain Emotional pain Loneliness Isolation	Alienation Confusion Fear
Assumptions	God is good to those who are good and judges those who are bad. Suffering is the result of sin.	
New Information	God's ways are not man's ways. God is sovereign in all that He determines. Suffering is not always the result of sin.	
Reappraisal	God is present in all suffering and vindicates the righteous. His presence is sufficient. There is meaning in suffering.	

Figure 10.1: Reframing the Trauma of Job

THE EFFECTS OF TRAUMA OBSERVED IN THE LIFE OF DAVID

David was the greatest king of Israel. He was one of the most gifted and versatile individuals in the Old Testament, rising out of obscurity to become Israel's most notable poet, musician, warrior, prophet, and king.[7]

David served as Israel's second monarch of the consolidated kingdom. His reign lasted for nearly forty years. During his reign, Israel established its power and influence throughout the eastern Mediterranean region and beyond, extending from the tribal area of Judah in Palestine west to the Nile River of Egypt and east to the Mesopotamian valley.

Coming to power as the king "after God's own heart" (1 Sam. 13:13–14; cf. Acts 13:22), David eventually came to realize that God had uniquely chosen him to establish an eternal kingdom (1 Sam. 16; 2 Sam. 7, 22; Ps. 18). In this respect, David plays an integral role in the lineage of Jesus.

The Old Testament prophets and the writers of the Gospels often refer to David. The author of at least seventy-three psalms, David reflects the heart of a faithful man whose vital relationship with God overflowed in his life despite his own traumatic experiences and personal failures.[8]

The Value of Understanding Trauma in David's Life

The value of David's life for understanding trauma and suffering lies in his constructive ability to trust God in multiple adverse and difficult circumstances. Some of David's pain resulted from his own sinful decisions, but some of it was due to no fault of his own. How David responded to trauma is instructive. The way he responded has been the source of comfort and inspiration for countless individuals throughout the ages. In the section below, we'll consider several traumatic events in David's life, and his responses to suffering and adversity when Saul pursued him.

The Traumatic Experiences of David

Jealousy can lead to rage. The success of David on the battlefield endeared David to the masses but incited jealousy and anger in Saul (1 Sam. 18:6–15). At least three times, David evaded Saul's direct attempt on his life, and eventually David had to flee. In 1 Samuel 18:1–31:13, the historical account describes the cat and mouse game that ensued between Saul and David, culminating in the death of Saul.

The account provides the historical backdrop for at least eight psalms that David wrote. In these psalms, we observe the heart and mind of David, and we discover how he was able to cope with trauma.

Saul recognized God's special relationship with David and the love that his daughter, Michal, had for David (1 Sam. 18:28), but he remained fearful of David and was "David's enemy continually" (1 Sam. 18:29). This fearful jealousy incited Saul to jeopardize David's life by placing him in untenable combat situations.

Saul directed his military staff to have David killed in battle. Eventually Saul's murderous jealousy and rage divided his family, pitting Saul's son, Jonathan, against David and destroying the marriage of his daughter. Confident of God's calling, David nevertheless ran for his life, fearful and untrusting of those aligned with Saul.

David became a national hero but pretended insanity in Gath to escape death. For a time he lived in a cave and gathered around himself all who were distressed, indebted, and embittered. He became a captain over them. He feared for his family and asked the king of Moab to provide asylum for them. After Saul killed the priests at Nob, David suffered from grief, blaming himself for their deaths. David was constantly on the run, hiding wherever he could find safety, whether it was in the deserts, in the mountains, or in the forests. Finally, given the opportunity to take Saul's life, David refused. He would not lift his hand against God's anointed.

However, David continued to fear Saul and fled to Philistia, where he made numerous raids against the neighboring tribes. Upon his return to the village of Ziglag, where he had lived, he found it burned to the ground and his wives and children missing. His men turned against him, blaming him for it and threatening to kill him. But as the Scriptures report, he found solace and strength in the Lord his God (1 Sam. 30:6).

In the chart below, I show how David reframed his experiences with the information provided in the psalms that correlated to the historical situation.

Psalm	The Historical Situation and Emotional State	New Information from the Psalm	Reframed Narrative
Ps. 59	1 Samuel 19:11: "His house is encircled by his enemies." Although he is innocent, he fears for his life; he feels maligned, assailed, and attacked.	God is the God of Israel and he is strong. God laughs at David's enemies. God is my fortress.	"I will triumph in the strength, love, and protection of God."
Ps. 56	1 Samuel 21:10: "David flees to Gath." He is oppressed, trampled upon, and afraid. He fears for his life.	God is trustworthy. God protects. God is for me.	"I will put my trust in God and I will not fear what man can do to me. I will fulfill my vows."
Ps. 34	1 Samuel 21:13: "David pretends to be insane." David feels impoverished and troubled. He is brokenhearted and afflicted.	God answers prayer. God delivers. God is good. God favors the righteous. God cares for the broken.	"I know the good are often afflicted but God is near to those who fear him and delivers the brokenhearted."
Ps. 142	1 Samuel 22:1: "David escapes to the cave of Adullam." He desires mercy from God. His spirit faints within; he feels trapped, abandoned, and forsaken.	God listens to my pain. God knows about my trouble. God is my refuge.	"Though no one cares, God cares, knows, and understands, and will deal bountifully with me."

Figure 10.2: Reframing the Trauma of David

Psalm	The Historical Situation and Emotional State	New Information from the Psalm	Reframed Narrative
Ps. 52	1 Samuel 22:9: "David is betrayed by Doeg, the Edomite." David senses those who plot against him. He is cognizant of their deceit and evil intent.	God's love is steadfast and endures. God judges the evil man.	"God honors me when I make him my refuge and when I put my trust in his steadfast love."
Ps. 54	1 Samuel 23:19: "David is betrayed by the Ziphites." David pleads for deliverance. He fears for his life.	God is my helper. He upholds my life. He will put an end to evil men.	"God always helps the righteous and delivers him. He will deal with the evil person."
Ps. 57	1 Samuel 24:1: "David flees from Saul, in the cave, when he was in the wilderness of Engedi." He fears imminent destruction. His soul is "bowed down" and in the "midst of lions."	God fulfills his purposes for me. He will deliver me and shame those who are against me. God is faithful and loving.	"God is faithful and loving, and fulfills his purposes in those whose heart is steadfast."
Ps. 7	1 Samuel 24:9: "David objects to the words of men who were with Saul." David is wrongly accused. He feels like his pursuers will tear his soul apart, and there is no one who will deliver him.	God judges righteously. God is my shield and protector. He judges evil.	"God will protect the upright in heart but judges the wicked."

Figure 10.2 (cont.): Reframing the Trauma of David

THE EFFECTS OF TRAUMA OBSERVED IN THE LIFE OF PAUL

We learn a lot more about suffering and trauma when we examine the life of the Apostle Paul. Several major sections of the New Testament address the Pauline doctrine of suffering (Rom. 8:18–39;

2 Cor. 1:3–11, 4:1–5:10, 11:16–12:10). In the sections below, we'll explore these passages.

Present Provisions and Future Glory

Romans 8:18–25 presents suffering and trauma in a temporal light, compared to the glorious future that awaits all believers. Even creation itself waits eagerly, longing for release from its "bondage to decay" when God will reconcile the world to himself and bring to completion his grand scheme of redemption (v. 21). Along with creation, believers will be transformed, receiving as their hope the "adoption as sons, the redemption of [the body]" (v. 23).[9]

Besides the hope that sustains us through suffering, we also have the help of the Holy Spirit, who "intercedes . . . with groanings too deep for words" (8:26). In our weakness, we are limited in understanding how to pray. But the Spirit knows what we need and prays for us in accord with the will of God (8:26–27). Theologian Karl Barth states: "[God] makes himself our advocate with himself that he utters for us that ineffable groaning, so that he will surely hear what we ourselves could not have told him, so that he will accept what he himself has to offer."[10]

In verses 28–30, Paul explains the position believers have before God. He views this position first from the perspective of the believer, then from the perspective of God. To love God is to know that God is at work in our lives to bring about good. This work of God for good is his work of conforming us to the "image of his Son" (v. 29). It can be inferred from the context that "all things" include suffering.[11] God uses suffering to bring us into conformity with the image of his Son. For this reason, we can "rejoice in our sufferings, knowing that suffering produces endurance, and endurance produces character, and character produces hope" (Rom. 5:3–4).

From God's perspective, believers are those who have been called according to God's purpose, a purpose that includes being "predestined to be conformed" to Christ (Rom. 8:29). "[A]nd those whom he has called are also justified; and those whom he has justified he has also glorified" (8:30b). The work of God for good is a work that brings to completion the work of salvation, from calling to justification to glorification. All of these aspects of God's work fulfill God's purposes.[12] Suffering then is one aspect of God's dealings with us in the larger effort of bringing us into conformity with Christ and fitting us for the glory that follows.[13]

Despite suffering, we can be assured God has a purpose for our suffering. This assurance is cast in the context of the cross, the means God used to satisfy the penalty and guilt of sin. Christ willingly gave his life to remove the charges that were leveled against us (Col. 2:13–14). Therefore, Paul concludes, "Who is to condemn? Christ Jesus is the one who died—more than that, who was raised— who is at the right hand of God, who indeed is interceding for us" (Rom. 8:34). Christ's sacrifice achieved so much more than what would have been achieved without his suffering and death. Christ's sacrifice removed all condemnation and provided for our advocacy, the living Lord who intercedes on our behalf. That is tremendous news. Despite all the pain, both Christ's and ours, nothing will ever separate us from God's prevailing love for us.

God used the suffering of Christ to bring about a greater good— our salvation. In a similar way, whatever tribulation we face, whatever trauma we may suffer, we can be confident that God's purposes will be fulfilled for our ultimate benefit, in keeping with his love for us, and for his glory and praise (Rom. 8:35, 37).[14] The experience of suffering does not change our position before God or his affection for us. While God uses suffering in our lives for various reasons, believers must remember that God never stops loving his children.

The Comfort of God

In 2 Corinthians, Paul states, "For as we share abundantly in Christ's sufferings, so through Christ we share abundantly in comfort too" (1:5). The comfort he speaks of is the comfort extended by God. In the context of our sufferings, we can rest in the comfort, support, and strength that "the God of all comfort" provides, commensurate with the sufferings we may experience. To the extent that we suffer, God grants equal comfort.

The passage outlines two parallel activities: (1) sharing in the sufferings of Christ and (2) sharing in the comfort of God. Paul expands on this when he states, "Indeed, we felt that we had received the sentence of death. But that was to make us rely not on ourselves but on God who raises the dead" (1:9). Suffering causes the sufferer to turn to God.

Paul was confident that the dual experiences of suffering and God's comfort would mean the experience of Christ's strength and the continued revitalization of those to whom he ministered.[15] The experience of God's comfort enables its recipients to extend this comfort to others in affliction. These recipients become indebted not only to God, who gives his comfort, but to others who are in need of that comfort as well.[16]

The Power and Glory of God

In 2 Corinthians 4:1–5:10, Paul contrasts his experience of suffering with the power and glory of God. Whatever one might experience in this life pales in significance when one considers the glory of the next life. If sufferings were to be weighed on a scale, the future glory of the believer would far outweigh the temporal and painful experiences of this life. Paul writes, "For this light momentary affliction is preparing for us an eternal weight of glory beyond all comparison" (4:17). The Hebrew word for glory is *kabod*, which means "heavy." In ancient days, those who were "glorious" were those who were wealthy or heavy in monetary coinage. So the future glory of the believer is a weighty glory, a substantial and marvelous experience that cannot compare to one's present experience of suffering. But there's more to it. Paul says one's present affliction also substantially contributes to their future glory. One's present affliction is like a monetary deposit, building spiritual wealth in future glory. The degree of one's suffering and perhaps how one responds to that suffering is determining in some way the degree of glory, when each will receive their reward.

The presence of God's power and the reality of the glorious gospel, culminating in heavenly realities, highlight the resiliency Paul continually demonstrated in the face of overwhelming obstacles. He was able to resist defeat by discovering several important lessons:

- His suffering was not about himself but about the expression of God's power and the furtherance of the gospel.

- His suffering revealed the life of Jesus in himself and in others.

- Future glory tempers all present suffering.

- External troubles made him dependent upon God and stronger within.

Of note, according to M. J. Harris in the *Expositor's Bible Commentary*, "He apparently saw ... a proportional relation between his 'death' and the 'life' of the Corinthian believers. The deeper his experience of … trials and sufferings … the richer their experience of the joys and privileges of Christian existence."[17] The way believers deal with suffering profoundly affects others. Just as Paul's experience enriched the Corinthians, so our experience with suffering can enrich the lives of others. Moreover, we discover from Paul that the mounting sufferings we may experience are actually light and temporary compared to the eternal weight of glory that awaits us. Finally, it would seem, the greater the affliction suffered, the greater the glory produced.[18]

Paul's Understanding of the Purpose of Suffering

In 2 Corinthians 11:16–12:10, the context for Paul's discussion of suffering is the defense of his apostleship against the charges leveled by false apostles. They said he was an idle boaster and sought only glory for himself.[19] But God had used Paul mightily and had chosen him to receive special revelations.

Beginning in verse 24 of chapter 11, Paul lists numerous trials he had experienced. They are listed as credentials of being a servant of Christ. The inference is that suffering is normative for those who wish to be a servant of Christ (cf. 1 Pet. 2:18–24). Paul shifts the focus away from himself to Christ. If he would boast about anything, it would not be about his position or his revelations but about his weaknesses, his sufferings. He does this to remind his readers of the sufficiency of Christ. Whatever we might accomplish for Christ is what Christ will accomplish through us and in us.

In chapter 12, he describes a "thorn in the flesh" he received from God as a way of reminding him of his own inadequacy. It was apparently a very serious and painful thing, some type of physical or mental ailment that persisted over a period of time. He prayed repeatedly that God would remove it.[20] But God did not remove it, lest Paul succumb to the temptation to boast about his apostleship or his privileges. Paul writes, "So to keep me from being too elated by the surpassing greatness of the revelations, a thorn was given me in the flesh, a messenger of Satan to harass me, to keep me from being too elated" (12:7).

Paul did nothing wrong to deserve this suffering. Nevertheless, God allowed it to prevent the sin of pride arising in Paul. It's also worth noting that while God permits this suffering, the immediate cause is attributed to a "messenger of Satan."[21] God is never the agent of evil.

God likewise permitted this suffering so that Paul might discover God's sufficiency (12:8–9). In Paul's extremity and difficulty, God revealed his grace and supplied what Paul needed.

Finally, God allowed Paul to suffer that he might experience the power of Christ in his life (12:9). His infirmity was a daily reminder of his inadequacy, of his inability to do God's work in his own strength. He had to rely on God.[22] When Paul was able to grasp the purpose of his suffering, the means that God sovereignly used to humble him, he gladly accepted what God desired. His weakness and his infirmity became not liabilities but assets, an avenue of divine strength (12:9–10). Paul concludes, "Therefore I will boast all the more gladly of my weaknesses, so that the power of Christ may rest upon me. For the sake of Christ, then, I am content with weaknesses, insults, hardships, persecutions, and calamities. For when I am weak, then I am strong" (12:9b–10).

Traumatic Events	The thorn in the flesh.
Traumatic Effects	Felt harassed. Felt insulted. Felt weak.
Assumptions	God would deliver him from this trial.
New Information	God's grace is sufficient and His power is made perfect in weakness.
Reappraisal	Paul boasted all the more gladly in his weaknesses. For when he was weak, then he was strong.

Figure 10.3: Reframing the Trauma of Paul — 2 Corinthians 12

NOTES

1. William P. Mahedy, "Some Theological Perspectives on PTSD," *National Center for PTSD Clinical Quarterly* 5, no. 1 (1995): 6–7.
2. Pentecost, *Man's Problems*.
3. Laney, *God*.
4. Pentecost, *Man's Problems*.
5. Ibid.
6. Ibid. See also Job 42:5.
7. W. A. Elwell, "David," in *Baker Encyclopedia of the Bible* Vol. 1, 581–586.
8. Ibid.
9. Everett Harrison, "Romans," in *The Expositor's Bible Commentary* vol. 10, ed. F. E. Gaebelein (Grand Rapids, MI: Zondervan, 1976).
10. As cited in Harrison, "Romans," 96.
11. Ibid.
12. Ibid.
13. Pentecost, *Man's Problems*.
14. Harrison, "Romans."
15. M. J. Harris, "II Corinthians," in *The Expositor's Bible Commentary* Vol. 10.
16. Ibid.
17. Ibid., 343.
18. Ibid.
19. Pentecost, *Man's Problems*.
20. Ibid.
21. Harris, "II Corinthians."
22. Pentecost, *Man's Problems*.

CHAPTER 11

RESILIENCE AND SPIRITUAL COPING

I've looked at life and realized that no matter what life hands you, because you can't control that, just take it by storm and strive on and have that attitude that you don't want to give up, so persevere and strive on.

—Jessica Lynch

R EADERS may recall the story of Private First Class Jessica Lynch, who was captured by Iraqi forces just three days after the start of the Iraq War. Her convoy was ambushed in Nasiriyah, Iraq, and several Soldiers, including a close friend, were killed in the attack. Just nineteen years old at the time, Jessica, badly injured, was taken prisoner by the Iraqis and later sexually assaulted. On April 1, 2003, nine days later, U.S. Special Operations forces dramatically rescued her.[1]

Since 2003, Jessica has been recovering from her injuries. After multiple surgeries and years of physical therapy, she still struggles physically but remains resilient. Although she wears a leg brace and often thinks about the attack, she has not let her traumatic experience control her or keep her from moving on with her life. In an interview with ABC News, she stated, "It's an everyday remembering. I mean I wake up, and I look at the injuries. Putting on the brace in the morning—you know all of that takes me back to that day. But I do. I wake up, I think to myself, you know what, I'm so lucky and blessed to have gotten to come home and rescued and made [sic] it out of there alive."[2]

Today, Jessica is a mom and a college graduate. She plans to continue her education with a master's in communication, and maybe a doctorate later. And her message to veterans is to persevere; don't quit.[3]

There are many similar stories of people who faced extraordinary circumstances and recovered. They did not let their traumatic experience rob them of a life. Elizabeth Smart is another familiar story. In 2002 at the age of fourteen, Elizabeth was abducted from her bedroom. Enduring multiple rapes and threats to her life, she was held hostage for nine months. In the years that followed her rescue, she married and wrote a book about her ordeal to help others know they don't have to let their lives become defined by the things that happen to them. People can recover and move on with their lives. They can be happy.[4]

Resilience gave Jessica and Elizabeth the ability to survive and later thrive. Resilience not only provided a protective shield for them but also a stimulus to rebound. It enabled them to recover and contributed to their emotional and mental growth.

But how resilience operates in a person is not a simple matter. Human beings are complex organisms. We can't necessarily point to a traumatic event like Elizabeth's abduction or Jessica's capture and conclude these events made them resilient. No. They obviously already possessed qualities that contributed to their ability to bounce back from adversity. But it's safe to say that their experiences made them more resilient.

THE MEANING OF RESILIENCE

Resilience is a learned behavior involving both thoughts and actions, and includes a process of rapid adaptation in the face of dire circumstances, trauma, general adversity, and other sources of stress.[5] Adaptation is evident when the person sufficiently recovers and returns to their original level of functioning.

Resilience is about the ability of an object to regain its shape after being bent, stretched, or compressed. Take, for example, the properties of an aluminum soda can. It's not very resilient—apply a little pressure and you've dented the can. But a Styrofoam coffee cup has some give to it. Squeeze the cup a little and maybe you'll spill some coffee. But relax the pressure and the cup regains its original shape. Similarly, resilience is evident in people who are flexible, capable of adjusting to their environment and returning to normal functioning.

Jessica and Elizabeth are just two examples of people who bounced back from adversity. They possessed certain qualities that enabled them to face adversity and win, qualities like flexibility, determination, and optimism. Their resilience reestablished normal functioning for them. They not only recovered, they advanced themselves beyond where they were before.[6]

Again we are reminded of what the Apostle Paul had in mind when he instructed, "More than that, we rejoice in our sufferings, knowing that suffering produces endurance and endurance produces character, and character produces hope" (Rom. 5:3–4). The presence of resilience contributes to personal development and leads to a change in perspective.

Emotional Connections

According to Susan Johnson in *The Practice of Emotionally Focused Couple Therapy: Creating Connection*, resilience is also about the quality of a person's emotional and social connections. It's not about the amount of adversity or stress someone goes through, it's about the presence of social connections and how these connections contribute to one's ability to cope effectively with adversity.[7] In research conducted on burn victims to determine who might develop PTSD, it was found that those who possessed strong emotional connections with family, community, and God were more resilient than those who had weaker connections. My research on combat veterans points to the strong influence of friends and family on the resilience of combat warriors.

Even strangers contribute to a servicemember's resilience. You don't have to personally know someone to benefit from your connection to them. I witnessed this in Iraq. Soldiers received care packages from churches, cards from school children, and letters from total strangers who just wanted to express their support. These were meaningful expressions of kindness that contributed to the well-being of our Soldiers and conveyed a positive message of support.

A Warrior's Resilience

There are several critical attitudes and skills that foster a warrior's resilience and help mitigate the development of PTS after battle. This resilience is manifested in warriors through the proper expression of attitudes, values, skills, discipline, and professionalism. While these do not make the servicemember "bulletproof," they contribute to a positive mind-set and reduce the likelihood of long-lasting debilitating effects such as chronic PTSD.

THE SOLDIER'S CREED AND ETHOS

The Soldier's Creed is a statement of faith; at best, it's what Soldiers believe about who they are, what they aspire to be, and what they resolve to do. At the least, it is the military institution's statement, crafted to instill identity, purpose, and value. Incorporated in the creed is the Warrior's Ethos, which encapsulates the ideals and values of the military profession. Warrior Ethos is an attitude of affirmation of conscience. It imbues the warrior with the proper warrior spirit, a spirit that affirms life over death, liberty over tyranny, and justice over oppression. It guides Soldiers in all their actions and serves as a moral compass that affirms the role of military members in the work of confronting evil. For a Soldier, the Warrior's Ethos means: "I will always place the mission first, never accept defeat, never quit, and never leave a fallen comrade behind."[8] The internalization of the Warrior Ethos strengthens Soldiers in their mission. It contributes to a Soldier's sense of purpose. It motivates each Soldier to pursue service to others over self and to strive for excellence in every endeavor.

VALUES AND SKILLS

In addition to the Soldier's Creed and Warrior Ethos, the inculcation of professional values, such as loyalty, duty, and respect, and interpersonal skills through resiliency programs contributes to the warrior's resilience. The development of resilience that supports the Soldier before, during, and after the battle is encompassed in the Army's

Comprehensive Soldier Fitness program. The program focuses on five pillars of fitness: family, social, physical, emotional, and spiritual. Master resiliency trainers are formally trained in resilience and assigned to units to assist in the development of these pillars of fitness, supported by other agencies including the Chaplaincy, Army Community Service, and Army Substance Abuse Program. The other Military Services have similar programs and agencies that support resilience as well.

DISCIPLINE

Discipline also contributes to a warrior's resilience. It's discipline that keeps an army from becoming a mob that rape and pillages or kills indiscriminately. Discipline, accompanied by values and moral leadership training, builds a force for good. During my tour in Iraq, despite our ongoing security mission, we were engaged in many humanitarian projects, from distributing soccer balls and school supplies to construction projects. On any given day, a servicemember might distribute sports equipment at a local school and later respond to an IED attack. Every servicemember had to maintain a high level of situational awareness, regardless of what they were doing.

How does a servicemember operate this way? How does a warfighter switch gears between humanitarian efforts and security operations, in which he might have to use his weapon? Discipline. It is a credit to all servicemembers that they are able to make this transition without loss of discipline. Units that are disciplined do this effectively. It is that learned discipline that keeps a servicemember from using his warrior skills inappropriately later.

PROFESSIONALISM

The military is a profession of arms and a societal institution that is guided by an ethical code. Professionalism builds confidence and contributes to resilience. As professionals, military members are formally steeped in values, traditions, and practices that contribute to the military's institutional authority and place in society. The military's role is defined not only by the Constitution, government, and military leaders, but also by society itself. The American people sanction the role of the American military, and through congressional representation send servicemembers to war.

The professional military ethic guides the actions of our servicemembers. It enables and prepares servicemember to do their work—combat as well as humanitarian operations. To the extent a warrior is prepared for military tasks, to that degree they are "battle proofed" against the detrimental effects of wartime trauma. At least, that is how it is supposed to work. The better prepared and indoctrinated, the less likely a servicemember develops post-combat stress.

But ethical indoctrination is not enough. Training in values and skills is not enough. It takes a solid moral foundation, one that is also informed by religion. Indeed, the professional military ethic is not based solely on social values and laws, it's informed by the tenets of religion like the Golden Rule (Matt. 7:12).[9]

There is a convergence of many factors that either protect the warrior or predict negative outcomes. But the development and maintenance of an ethos, values, skills, discipline, and professionalism have tremendous value. They enable warriors to execute their mission with minimal post-combat effects.

WARRIOR TRAINING

Training prepares the servicemember technically, tactically, and personally for the rigors and uncertainty of combat. While operational planning is used extensively to prepare the warfighter for combat, many other things occur in combat that are not addressed in the operational plan. These may have significant impact on the servicemember.

The presence of change and uncertainty are significant factors of stress. Adapting to change, remaining flexible, and leveraging resources will help the warrior reduce stress levels. There is always a lot of uncertainty in battle that contributes to fear. Servicemembers must learn to manage their fears. In combat, the warfighter must remain on constant alert or suffer the consequences of complacency. This state of constant alertness takes its toll on the body, and so servicemember must learn how to manage. Identifying and implementing an effective sleep plan helps.

The battlefield is a horrible place. Warriors must be prepared for the sights, sounds, and smells. Knowing what to expect will help the servicemember who is faced with the reality of combat. Being physically, mentally, and spiritually fit prepares the servicemember. Servicemembers who are spiritually trained do better in combat.

REALISTIC TRAINING

Tough, realistic training prepares servicemembers for the unpredictability of the battlefield. If conducted correctly, training reduces the likelihood of severe post-traumatic stress developing later. It builds confidence by contributing to technical proficiency, reliance upon equipment, and trust among members of the team. Training develops and hones warrior tasks and drills. Servicemember are always training. Training that mimics the sights and sounds of the battlefield ensures success in combat when it counts.

All realistic training includes stress inoculation. The most elite combat forces today immerse themselves in training that taxes the tactical capabilities of their units and the technical, mental, physical, and emotional capabilities of their servicemembers. Any effective military training creates stress through shared hardship, various forms of deprivation, and intense technical and physical demands.

The Army routinely sends units to the National Training Center at Fort Irwin, California, to test their mettle and hone their skills in extreme environmental conditions. The center subjects them to almost incessant mission scenarios executed by a savvy opposing force that puts pressure on a unit's capabilities and vulnerabilities. This is done not only to make them more effective, but also to subject every Soldier to increased stress so that they learn about their own limits and capabilities.[10]

Stress inoculation not only builds confidence, it works as a tremendous learning tool, providing scenarios that teach the servicemember what to expect in battle and how to react to the enemy. Tested units challenge the capabilities of teams. Shared hardship builds the teams.

Realistic training includes the use of after-action reviews (AARs) to evaluate actions and reactions and to enable the warfighter to make corrections. AARs are invaluable. They instill confidence and contribute immensely to learning. Lieutenant Colonel Dave Grossman, while affirming the use of AARs, argues for the use of critical incident stress debriefings after combat actions. He also recommends learning to use tactical breathing as a way of lowering the heart rate and improving effectiveness.[11]

Tactical breathing is an effective means of reducing stress, improving focus, and minimizing negative emotional or behavioral reactions. It is a four-count breathing technique in which a person breathes in deeply and exhales slowly. It is done by exercising the diaphragm in the inhalation process, involving long, controlled breaths through the nose, and exhaling through the mouth. Athletes, speakers, and performers use tactical breathing to stave off fear or nervousness and gain control or sustain good tone. My wife is a musician and experiences a lot of nervousness when she performs. To deal with her nervousness, she uses tactical breathing, and it helps her.

Debriefings

Debriefing after critical incidents involves a process that helps a group, such as a squad, discuss what actually happened and identify each member's respective role in the incident. It is a way of checking thoughts, emotions, and actions. The process gives perspective on the event by solidifying the facts. As each member of the squad shares her or his perceptions, the group is able to gain a more accurate picture of what actually happened. It's not unusual for members of the squad to have a distorted or incomplete perception of the event. Going through the event methodically within forty-eight to seventy-two hours after an incident is one of the best ways of mitigating the occurrence of post-traumatic stress.

The practice of debriefing prepares warriors for the potential effects of stress, gives them an opportunity to address stress before it becomes disruptive, and helps participants normalize the feelings and thoughts that the group may have. The normalization of thoughts and feelings is an important element in this process. These things, taken together, lessen the pain and help reduce the likelihood of post-traumatic stress.[12]

There are several models of critical incident stress debriefings currently being used in the military. The Mitchell Model, which I have used, is a specific, seven-step crisis intervention process intended for small groups to address a specific traumatic event or critical incident.[13] The goal of the debriefing is to clarify the event and reduce the stress in homogeneous groups, to enhance unit cohesion and performance. It's not a one-size-fits-all approach to every critical incident, but I have used it effectively in combat when dealing with Soldiers who have experienced a traumatic event.

MENTORSHIP

Training involves mentorship, particularly in the development of younger servicemembers. Through mentorship, younger members of the profession learn the art of war. The presence of mature, seasoned warriors in training and on the battlefield is a calming influence. It induces rationality, reduces fear, and affirms the warrior in his tasks. An all-volunteer force is exceptionally prepared to inculcate its new members in the art of war and the tenets of its profession, because no one coerced any member to join. The older, more experienced officer or noncommissioned officer trains the younger, less experienced officer or enlisted member. Any brand-new second lieutenant or ensign soon recognizes the value of a wise and experienced senior NCO and listens to their advice.

Mentorship contributes to a more experienced force, a force that is better prepared to deal with the stresses of combat. If so prepared, members of the force are less vulnerable to the development of PTS. In short, the military creates a more resilient force by leveraging the skills and knowledge of its most seasoned veterans.

COMMUNITY AFFIRMATION

It is the community that sends our servicemembers to war. The community's affirmation is critical to sustaining the warfighter after combat. Our servicemembers need to know the community is behind them. While not everyone is suited to serve as society's protectors, some are, such as our servicemembers, law enforcement officials, and emergency first responders. They are prepared to protect the community. As someone observed, "People sleep peacefully in their beds only because rough men stand ready to do violence on their behalf."[14] It is appropriate that they should do so.

Think back to 9/11. Remember the exploits and courage of the first responders who ran up the stairs of those burning buildings while others were running down to safety? They, along with our servicemembers and law enforcement members, are the protectors of society, the ones who "stand in the gap" and keep watch over the rest of us.[15]

Who are these servants of society? They are men and women who run to the sound of the guns, who run into the flames to save us. Like Nehemiah's men, they guard the gates of the city and stand watch on the wall. They are the heroes of our community. It is the community's responsibility to accept its role in sending them out.

Moreover, it is the community's responsibility to affirm the warrior in the business of killing. This was the problem with returning Vietnam veterans. Society abdicated its role. The community failed to affirm our veterans; instead, the community attacked them and shamed them for what society had sent them to do. When the community accepts its role in war and affirms the warrior in his or her tasks, it is contributing to the well-being of the warrior and their ability to reintegrate into society.

Just War Theory and Killing

Warriors who possess a sound understanding of just war theory and killing are better prepared to deal with the reality of combat and its effects on them.[16] The theory of just war assumes a legitimate basis for war, a just cause. A just war must be properly authorized. Governments or international governing bodies, in concert with sovereign states, possess the legitimate authority to wage war. Nations have the right to self-defense and the responsibility to protect their citizens.

American servicemembers are taught about the nature of combat and the reasons for war. Since war inevitably involves taking human life, sometimes—innocent life, the theory of war can seem confusing and lead to uncertainty. Servicemembers need to know why killing is sometimes necessary and appropriate. They need to understand the moral authority they've been granted to take life. But war must only be pursued as a measure of last resort, when all other measures have failed.

American warfighters are trained to kill discriminately and only when necessary. Just war theory addresses actions taken in war. There are three critical components to this aspect of the theory:

- Discrimination—servicemembers must only engage legitimate targets.

- Restraint—warriors must exercise restraint in their use of force, the appropriate degree of force necessary to achieve the desired outcome. This is also referred to as the principle of proportionality.

- Double effect—the acknowledgment that civilian deaths will occur in war as the result of legitimate actions.

The Scriptures contain the prohibition, "Thou shalt not kill" (Exod. 20:13 KJV). It is actually a prohibition against murder, and rightly translated should read, "Thou shalt not murder." It's possible to commit murder in a war, and unfortunately it happens. Most recently (as of this writing), Staff Sergeant Robert Bales was sentenced to life in prison without parole for murdering sixteen Afghan civilians.

It is possible to murder enemy combatants when they have surrendered or when they have been incapacitated. During my tour in Iraq, one of our Soldiers shot and killed an injured, incapacitated enemy combatant. It is an unfortunate occurrence in war, and it happens on all sides.

Killing is a hard thing. Humans have a natural aversion to killing. In research conducted by S. L. A. Marshall and discussed in *Men Against Fire*, he found most people resist killing. His surveys of Soldiers during World War II and Korea revealed that most Soldiers never fired their weapons while engaged with the enemy or never aimed their weapons at the enemy.[17]

The story of Alvin York may help us understand how to approach the problem of killing. Sergeant Alvin C. York was awarded the Medal of Honor for killing at least twenty-five German soldiers and capturing 132 more in the Argonne Forest during the waning days of World War I.[18] At first, when he was drafted, he contemplated claiming conscientious objector status because of his Christian beliefs. He wrote on his draft notice: "Don't want to fight." However, he eventually was convinced by his commanding officer that killing is sometimes necessary in war because of the moral authority that is given to each Soldier, the necessity of self-defense, and the concept of liberty that ensures the safety of all freedom-loving people. For York, it was a moral crisis that took a great deal of contemplation and prayer. But once he became convinced of the rightness of the cause in France, he was at peace with it. He went on to become one our nation's esteemed but reluctant heroes.

Whether we send our servicemembers to war because we cannot go or choose not to go, every American is responsible for sending them. And every American is responsible for the actions of our military in war. As a military chaplain, I am a noncombatant. I do not carry a weapon; I am not on the battlefield to kill the enemy. However, my presence on the battlefield is a powerful reminder to warfighters that they have the moral authority to kill the enemy. In a similar sense, the American public, through its representatives, gives servicemembers the moral authority for their actions in combat within the law.

Soldiers must come to terms with killing in order to engage in the business of killing. As professional servicemembers, we learn about the need for killing and its limits. Failure to become psychologically and spiritually prepared to take human life ensures severe psychological and spiritual damage later.[19] Pastors and chaplains can assist warfighters in coming to terms with killing. A healthy understanding of this important issue will sustain a servicemember in combat and minimize the likelihood of residual, detrimental issues developing in the servicemember after combat.

SPIRITUALITY AND RESILIENCE

Research supports the contribution of religion or spirituality to the development of resilience. The veteran is benefitted by an active faith life.[20] Some studies show that people who are spiritually engaged are healthier, more content, and better adjusted than those who are not so engaged.[21] In the sections below, we'll consider some of the ways spirituality or religion contribute to resilience.

THE ROLE OF FAITH

Having an active faith provides a person with the strong belief that she or he is part of a bigger story, a larger plan, and a greater purpose. Faith acknowledges God's control over circumstances. The experiences of trauma and pain are not the end of the story. Faith gives the traumatized person a framework for making meaning and finding purpose. Faith in a resilient person also provides a source of hopefulness about the future. Sometimes, like Job, when we're left with nothing, it is our faith in God that gets us through.

This was the situation with Lieutenant Colonel Donald "Digger" Odell when he found himself a POW in North Vietnam. When I asked him what really got him through his initial capture, torture, and then the five-and-a-half years he spent at the "Hanoi Hilton," he said it was his faith in God, especially the comfort he received from the words of Psalm 23, and then the support of fellow POWs.[22] He also said it didn't hurt to keep a sense of humor. Upon his return home in 1973, after a brief hospital stay for injuries he sustained as a prisoner, he dealt with symptoms of PTSD. He overcame them, in part, by sharing his story and putting his efforts into helping others. For the last thirty years he's shared his story with countless groups and has assisted with Special Olympics in the State of Michigan.

The biblical story of Joseph also illustrates how an active faith operates within a resilient person. Despite several significant traumatic experiences in his life—being abandoned by his brothers, sold as a slave, wrongly accused, and imprisoned unjustly—Joseph was able to acknowledge that though these experiences were meant for evil, God had used them for good (Gen. 45:4–15, 50:19–21). Furthermore, God used these experiences to prepare Joseph for future service. He was uniquely positioned to avert economic disaster and preserve his family.

The Apostle Paul, as we considered earlier, provides another example of how resilience operates in a spiritual individual (2 Cor. 4:7–18). Despite multiple setbacks, Paul was able to respond resiliently because he understood he was engaged in a larger task and a greater purpose with a brighter future. Paul focused on the task of preaching the gospel. It animated everything he did; nothing compared to it and nothing was more important. Nothing was going to stand in his way

(Phil. 1). He was singularly focused on fulfilling God's purposes for his life, despite persecution and imprisonment. At the end of his life, he reveled in the fact that he had fulfilled God's calling. He awaited a future reward with joy and anticipation (2 Tim. 4:6–8).

Active Spirituality

Active spirituality during combat and after combat is a resilience factor, promoting healing and recovery. Servicemembers who pray feel connected to God, possess a sense of God's presence and protection, and indicate spiritual activities continue to play a healing role after combat.[23]

Servicemembers who stop hating the enemy have proven to be receptive to God's mercy and forgiveness. The true-life stories of Ernest Gordon and Louis Zamperini, discussed earlier, illustrate the power of forgiveness and the wonder of God's mercy.

Spirituality tempers actions in combat. Warfighters who exercised restraint in combat, displayed mercy to the defenseless, and respected their opponent were better able to cope later with PTS.[24]

Religious Fellowships

Traumatized servicemembers who participate in religious fellowships report receiving effective support in dealing with PTS symptoms. These fellowships are safe havens for troubled souls. Simple actions that convey acceptance, trust, and support encourage members in these groups to share their burdens and open their hearts to the truths of God's Word.

The Power of Prayer

Prayer represents a spiritual connection to God and assists servicemembers with the stress of combat and its effects later. According to one Vietnam veteran, prayer helped him stay calm in battle, alleviated his fears, provided wisdom to make the right choices, and prevented him from pursuing self-serving things.[25] According to another veteran, prayer helped him avoid bitterness and hate; it gave him peace and perspective that made it easier to forgive. It also stimulated him to serve others more selflessly, and resulted in personal healing.[26]

Spiritual Values

In a survey conducted for this book, Soldiers were asked to assess the influence of their spiritual values on coping and on the development of resilience. Slightly more than half of the respondents indicated their spiritual values highly enabled them to cope with combat. Forty percent of the Soldiers surveyed also said spiritual values improved after combat, and only 16 percent said their values declined. When asked to identify the factors that contributed to the improvement in their spiritual values, servicemembers identified the support of friends and family as the most significant supporting factor contributing to their spiritual values.

In numerous interviews I conducted, Soldiers consistently reported faith, prayer, family support, and comradeship were the elements that most often contributed to their resilience and helped them cope with combat. These findings almost exactly corresponded to a survey I administered to 165 veterans who had returned from Iraq or Afghanistan.

Strength-based Approaches and Developing Resilience

The presence of strengths, whether derived from adversity or apart from it, has been shown to increase resilience and protect against the most damaging effects of PTS.[27]

Resilience-building conditions help people develop self-righting tendencies. Those who leverage their own resources are able to overcome adversity, such as abuse, poverty, and violence. Below, we'll look at some of the resources and factors that may be understood as strengths and that contribute to the development of resilience.

FAMILY STRENGTHS

Research over the last two decades on family systems demonstrates the efficacy of focusing on strengths and not on weaknesses. Studies indicate that resilient people possess certain strengths that help them survive and potentially grow. This was certainly evident in the stories of Jessica and Elizabeth.

In a study that assessed the strengths of 182 families in which the variables of risk, family strengths, and family functioning were tested, the presence of family strengths predicted higher levels of functioning despite the level of risk. Family strengths included insight, initiative, independence, creativity, social support, humor, and morality/spirituality.[28] The presence and the development of these strengths contribute to greater levels of functioning and the ability to bounce back quickly and easily from adverse situations.

PROTECTIVE FACTORS

Besides the presence of strengths, there are other factors that support the development of resilience. These include flexibility, appraisal, and social support.[29] People who are flexible, who are capable of looking at things from a variety of perspectives, and who enjoy social connections tend to function better in adverse situations than those who are rigid, tunnel-focused, and less connected or lacking social support. People who feel they have some degree of control over their lives, or possess a deep commitment to their activities, or generally positive toward change also respond better in adverse circumstances.[30]

Established Networks

Resilient people operate within established networks, where they regularly access resources, develop strong bonds of love and trust, and participate in communal rituals. A communal ritual may be as simple as taking meals together. The development and fostering of religious connections within a faith community, as well as with God, contribute to a person's resilience.[31] The presence of social support for trauma victims is a common theme in the development of resilience. This is particularly encouraging given that churches may provide a social outlet for veterans struggling to reconnect or find meaning in their lives.

History and Combat Exposure

Those who possess a history of success in overcoming challenges and who have learned from their adversity are more resilient than those who possess no history of success when facing hardship.[32] Researchers assessing the resilience of warriors found the experience of negative changes accompanies many positive benefits.[33] Glen Elder and Elizabeth Clipp, reporting on a study of resilience and the emotional health of veterans in the *Journal of Personality*, found positive early life experiences contributed to resilience in combat veterans. Those who experienced intense combat exposure adapted well, especially during periods between young adulthood and middle age.[34] They also found a correlation between the presence of emotional or behavioral problems in adolescence and a lower level of resilience at midlife. Overall, they concluded that (1) servicemembers were more resilient by adapting to adverse situations in combat and (2) resilience was a significant resource for these veterans.[35] While these conclusions are not earth shattering, this research among veterans is significant and demonstrates that combat exposure contributes to the development of resilience.

SHARED EXPERIENCES

Shared experiences contribute to a sense of connection and empowerment and support resilience. In a study conducted by Brené Brown on shame resilience theory, participants felt more connected because of shared power and empathy.[36] Having a renewed sense of connection comes from identifying with shared experiences, experiencing mutual support, and considering multiple options. A study has been published in the *Journal of Traumatic Stress* concerning women with a history of abuse as children and as adults. Results showed that these women experienced less severe symptoms of PTSD in the presence of significant levels of social support, particularly from those with similar stories.[37]

HUMANITARIAN ACTIONS

There is evidence that performing humanitarian acts during combat builds resilience in combat veterans. Servicemembers who engage in humanitarian acts during combat are less likely to suffer from the effects of post-traumatic stress after combat. While in Iraq, we engaged in humanitarian activities. I observed the calming and humanizing effect they had on Soldiers who participated. While the intent of these humanitarian actions was to support the Iraqi people, it is clear that they also benefited our Soldiers. Furthermore, acts of service and mercy tend to reverse the effects of hatred and initiate steps toward reconciliation between offended parties.[38]

Performing reparative acts during or after combat can aid in recovery. Some servicemembers who engage in these activities may feel they are atoning for their sins.[39] Their sense of atonement helps them let go of their hatred and accept God's mercy and forgiveness. Warriors who reflect upon their humanitarian or heroic acts are less likely to experience deep and lasting effects of post-traumatic stress. Their atoning efforts raise their level of hope for full restoration.[40]

RESILIENCE FACTORS IN COMBAT

In a study I conducted on resilience, 51 percent of the 165 Soldiers surveyed indicated a high appraisal of their resilience during combat. (Combat situations ranged from low to high intensity among the sampled population.) After combat, 21 percent indicated a decrease in resilience, 38 percent indicated an increase in resilience, and 41 percent indicated that they experienced no change in their resilience after combat. While these results are somewhat mixed and not conclusive, they do indicate that most of these combat veterans did not experience a decrease in resilience.[41]

More significantly, the study also assessed resilience factors that most supported servicemembers during combat. Across a domain of ten factors, servicemembers identified five that most strongly supported them during combat: 1) support of comrades, 2) home-front support, 3) religious beliefs, 4) teamwork, and 5) mission focus. Of the five factors, home-front support was the most frequently reported factor and the factor that most significantly supported resilience. While religious beliefs were not the most significant factor, religious beliefs were identified in the top five.[42] These findings correlate with similar findings that report on the power of connections. In addition, I suggest the factors that supported servicemembers during combat are the same factors that will contribute to their healing and recovery.

Resilience and Self-Concept

As we have learned, PTS affects a warrior's concept of self, deepening his or her sense of isolation and feelings of entrapment. Soldiers suffering from PTS can develop resilience by learning to perceive their situation from another's perspective. Gaining another person's perspective, in which the veteran can feel accepted, regarded without judgment, and understood emotionally and cognitively, can produce a sense of connection, power, and freedom in the veteran.[43]

The sense of isolation is deepened when a person experiences depersonalization and when there is a loss of self, safety, and predictability. Depersonalization is akin to loss of identity. It is sometimes associated with the feeling of being trapped, when the veteran feels like he or she has no options.[44] This reality may also explain the rise of suicide among returning combat veterans.

The effective use of groups in treatment, where facilitators leverage the positive perspectives of other members of the group, will mitigate the feelings of isolation in the veteran who is suffering with PTS. Groups develop members' resilience and contribute to a positive self-concept so necessary for the servicemember's healing.

Resilience and Comradeship

Comradeship contributes to resilience. There is a deep bond of intimacy formed among comrades in combat. In my research, Soldiers highly rated the significance of comradeship as a factor of resilience during combat. Our healthy connection to others enables us to withstand tremendous stress. In studies that were conducted among members of the Eighth Air Force during World War II, comradeship contributed to the resilience of aircrews.[45] Men were able to keep flying and fighting despite continual danger and loss of life. Only in

231

cases where members of the aircrew lost their closest friends was there an erosion of resilience.

Soldiers fight for each other. Larry Dewey in *War and Redemption* cites a study that was conducted in 1945 by two American psychiatrists, who published their experiences treating war casualties in *War Neuroses.*[46] In the last chapter of their book, they wondered why most Soldiers did not succumb to war anxiety. They concluded the reason was mainly *esprit de corps*. The bonds of love forged in the crucible of battle enabled warriors to sustain themselves. Strong leadership established on trust and respect, clear mission objectives, and a sense of invulnerability all contributed to servicemembers' resilience. Interestingly, the researchers also discovered the presence of a conscious hostility or revenge contributed to resilience among some of the warriors surveyed. I don't think this is unusual. Shared hatred of a common enemy contributes to camaraderie. But what happens later, after the bonds are broken and the effort concludes?

War, especially extended conflict, takes its toll on the human spirit. Unit identification disintegrates due to casualty replacements. The sight of friends wounded and killed creates intense grief. Soldiers eventually lose their sense of invulnerability and emotionally break.[47]

The loss of comradeship, unit cohesion, and a reason to fight reduces resilience. Removed from their combat units, camaraderie, and the tenuousness of war, servicemembers experience disillusionment, alienation, and lack of purpose. In this state, servicemembers experience an overwhelming realization of what they've done and what they've seen.[48]

NOTES

1. Angel Canales, "Pvt. Jessica Lynch, 10 Years After Iraq Rescue: Pain But Much Gain," *ABC News*, Sept. 19, 2013, accessed December 15, 2013, http://abcnews.go.com/US/bob-woodruff-talks-jessica-lynch-recovery-future-10/story?id=20304493.

2. Ibid.

3. Ibid.

4. A. Duke, "Elizabeth Smart Shares '100%' of Her Kidnapping Terror in Book," *CNN U.S*, October 8, 2013, accessed January 11, 2014, http://www.cnn.com/2013/10/07/us/elizabeth-smart-anderson-cooper/index.html.

5. M. Eberly, "Resiliency: Bouncing Back From Adversity."

6. Ibid. See also Leslie Morland, Lisa Butler, and Gregory Leskin, "Resilience and Thriving in a Time of Terrorism," in *Trauma, Recovery, and Growth*, 39-61; "Resilience," *The American Heritage Dictionary*; K. Reivich and A. Shatté, *The Resilience Factor* (New York: Broadway Books, 2002).

7. Susan Johnson, *The Practice of Emotionally Focused Couple Therapy: Creating Connection* (New York: Guilford, 1996).

8. See http://www.army.mil/. The Soldiers Creed: I am an American Soldier. I am a warrior and a member of a team. I serve the people of the United States, and live the Army Values. I will always place the mission first. I will never accept defeat. I will never quit. I will never leave a fallen comrade. I am disciplined, physically and mentally tough, trained and proficient in my warrior tasks and drills. I always maintain my arms, my equipment and myself. I am an expert and I am a professional. I stand ready to deploy, engage, and destroy, the enemies of the United States of America in close combat. I am a guardian of freedom and the American way of life. I am an American Soldier.

9. D. M. Snider and A. P. Shine, "A Soldier's Morality, Religion, and Our Professional Ethic: Does the Army's Culture Facilitate Integration, Character Development, and Trust in the Profession?" (Carlisle, PA: US Army War College Press, 2014).

10. See Grossman, *On Combat* for an extensive discussion.

11. Ibid.

12. Ibid.

13. See http://www.info-trauma.org/flash/media-e/mitchellCriticalIncidentStressDebriefing.pdf.

14. Attributed to Richard Grenier, http://quote.investigator.com/category/richard.genier/.

15. D. Grossman, *On Combat*.

16. For a thorough discussion of just war theory, I recommend two articles: John Buell, "Just War Theory and the Wars of the 20th Century," *Yale-New Haven Teachers Institute* (2002), accessed December 23, 2015, http://www.yale.edu/ynhti/curriculum/units/2002/3/; and M. B. Holmes, "Just War Theory and It's Applicability to Targeted Killing" (MS thesis, US Army Command and General

Staff College, 2011). See also Grossman, *On Killing*.

17. S. L. A. Marshall, Men Against Fire (New York: William Morrow, 1947).

18. R. G. Humble, *Sgt. Alvin C. York: A Christian Patriot* (Circleville, OH: Advocate Publishing House, 1966). Michael Birdwell, "Legends and Traditions of the Great War: Sergeant Alvin York," accessed December 26, 2015, http://www.worldwar1.com/heritage/sgtayork.htm.

19. Grossman, *On Combat*.

20. Plante, "What do the Spiritual."

21. Ibid. See also Schiraldi, *The Post-Traumatic*.

22. Author's interview with Lt. Col. (Ret.) Donald "Digger" Odell, USAF, on March 25, 2015.

23. Plante, "What do the Spiritual"; see also Dewey, *War and Redemption*.

24. Dewey, *War and Redemption*.

25. Ibid.

26. Ibid.

27. C. Lietz, "Uncovering Stores of Family Resilience: A Mixed Methods Study of Resilient Families, Part 1," *Families in Society: The Journal of Contemporary Social Services*, (2006): 575–581. See also G. O. Higgins, *Resilient Adults: Overcoming a Cruel Past* (San Francisco: Jossey-Bass, 1994).

28. Lietz, "Uncovering Stores."

29. Eberly, "Resiliency."

30. Ibid.

31. T. Waynick, P. Frederich, D. Scheider, R. Thomas, and G. Bloomstrom, "Human Spirituality, Resilience, and the Role of Military Chaplains" in *Military Life: The Psychology of Serving in Peace and Combat Vol. 2: Operational Stress*, ed. A. Adler, C. Castro, T. Britt (Westport, CT: Praeger Security International, 2006), 173–191

32. Ibid.

33. Glen Elder and Elizabeth Clipp, "Combat Experience and Emotional Health: Impairment and Resilience in Later Life," *Journal of Personality* 57, no. 2 (1989): 311–341.

34. Ibid.

35. Ibid.

36. Brown, "Shame Resilience Theory."

37. J. Schumm, M. Briggs-Phillips, and S. Hobfoll, "Cumulative Interpersonal Traumas and Social Support as Risk and Resiliency Factors in Predicting PTSD and Depression Among Inner-City Women," *Journal of Traumatic Stress* 19, no. 6 (2006): 825–836.

38. Dewey, *War and Redemption*.

39. Ibid.

40. Ibid. See also Brown, "Shame Resilience Theory."

41. Bonura, "A Biblical Approach."

42. Ibid.

43. Herman, *Trauma and Recovery*.

44. Matsakis, Post-traumatic.

45. Dewey, *War and Redemption*.
46. Ibid.
47. Ibid.
48. Ibid.

CHAPTER 12

POST-TRAUMATIC GROWTH

More than that, we rejoice in our sufferings, knowing
that suffering produces endurance, and endurance
produces character, and character produces hope.

—Romans 5:3–4

O N August 5, 2010, the San Jose gold and copper mine collapsed, trapping thirty-three Chilean miners 700 meters below the surface of the Atacama Desert near Copiapó, Chile. Only the winter before, the Chilean people had endured an 8.8-magnitude earthquake, leaving in its wake devastation, looting, and loss of life. But the collapse of the San Jose mine was different because it ended happily, uniting the Andean nation, igniting strong national pride, and strengthening its people.[1]

For seventeen long days, the miners sustained themselves on meager rations under limited lighting and cramped conditions before they made contact with the outside world. How did they survive? What kept them going for another fifty-two days before they were finally rescued? More significantly, how did most of them reenter the world changed and stronger? Yes, discipline, good order, and leadership contributed to their survival and prevented panic. But they also found strength through their faith in God and left the mine with newfound meaning and purpose for their lives. Their faith made them resilient in the face of trauma; they adapted, and they came out stronger.

Testimonies from the survivors suggest their experience gave them a brand-new perspective on life. It encouraged greater intimacy with God and a deeper resolve to live better and more productive lives.[2] According to several news reports, the men found unusual spiritual strength from their faith. There is no doubt their faith gave them the will to survive and that their ordeal contributed to personal and spiritual post-traumatic growth.

TRAUMA LEADS TO GROWTH

This story illustrates the truth that trauma leads to emotional and spiritual growth.[3] Not that long ago, clinicians typically used a disease model to understand trauma and its effects, focusing on what was wrong with the patient. But the assumptions of clinical psychology are changing from this medical model to a more positive, psychological perspective.[4] More and more clinicians are advocating this perspective on trauma.[5] Those who have a positive view of traumatic events seem to be less likely to report high levels of distress.[6]

Studies show many servicemembers, particularly those who have experienced a moderate level of wartime trauma, come through their traumatic experiences with a greater sense of purpose, a deeper appreciation for life, changed priorities, and in some cases a deeper desire to walk closer to God.[7]

In short, trauma and the crisis it creates for people do not have to lead to a bad end. A crisis can be a catalyst for positive change, creating opportunity and means for personal growth.[8]

POST-TRAUMATIC GROWTH

Post-traumatic growth, a term coined by University of North Carolina–Charlotte professors Richard Tedeschi and Lawrence Calhoun, represents a permanent advance beyond baseline functioning. While resilience may include elements of growth, the focus of resilience is on the ability to quickly bounce back from adversity and regain normal or baseline functioning. Post-traumatic growth differs from resilience because it represents a significant change in outlook. It's a measurable and positive advancement in emotional, mental, and spiritual aspects.[9] It's a reconfiguration of schema; that is, a person has adjusted her or his assumptions about the world, one's self, and the meaning assigned to events in a positive and helpful way.[10] This positive advancement and reconfiguration was certainly evident with the Chilean miners!

Given the opportunity to make adjustments to assumptions by acquiring new appraisals of trauma, victims learn to adjust their lives, changing how they think and feel about what has happened to them. This represents growth, and it indicates why cognitive reconstruction and reframing are significant. It's a clear shift from focusing on emotional states and subjective wellness to acquiring new constructs or enlarging the circle of assumptions, resulting in positive psychological well-being or emotional and spiritual growth.[11]

Growth occurs when the person is able to make sense of the event, manage emotions, and initiate action. In other words, as I stated earlier, once a person is able to assign meaning to their pain, that person begins to heal. The healing process implies growth. Eventually, the traumatized individual gains new insight through increased internalization of what has occurred. The person experiences a renewed appreciation for life and the development of wisdom.

Developed, Not Defined

Trauma either defines or develops a person. Growth is about development. Paul Cardall is a contemporary jazz pianist and one of my favorite musicians. He was born with a congenital heart defect and at that time was given only days to live. But Paul survived, enduring many surgeries and illnesses during his childhood. As a child, he learned to play the piano and found strength and comfort through music. Then, when he was in high school, one of his best friends was killed in a car accident. Out of his grief, Paul composed a musical tribute and went on to write a dozen more songs that were eventually produced as an album. Since the mid-1990s, Paul has composed more songs and released additional albums, including a musical adaptation of the best seller *The Christmas Box* and *Daily Devotions and Miracles: A Journey of Hope and Healing*, among others.

Why is this illustration significant? Paul is just one of many people in the world who decided that he would not become a victim of his illness or the tragedies in his life. He would rise above them and make a difference. Jessica Lynch and Elizabeth Smart, mentioned in chapter 11, were not only resilient, possessing the qualities that enabled them to resume normal functioning, they also grew from their traumatic experiences, developing themselves and making contributions to others. This is the nature of post-traumatic growth.

THE PROCESS OF POST-TRAUMATIC GROWTH

The process of post-traumatic growth begins with a significant traumatic event that challenges fundamental beliefs about the world. It develops with cognitive deliberation on the meaning of the event, which compels continued reflection. This results in internalization of the event and cognitive and behavioral adjustment.

But what is the catalyst for growth? How does the process begin? I believe the catalyst is cognitive reappraisal. It starts with the mind. When a victim of trauma reappraises the event, they engage in a deliberate effort to reconstruct an accurate narrative. They then look for new information that enables reframing of the event. Successfully doing that leads to healing, to newfound meaning, and finally to growth. Those who experience growth, particularly those who reframe their experience through religious information, report feelings of being closer to God and their church, reduced anxiety and depression, and a sense of greater personal meaning or purpose in life.[12]

DOMAINS OF POST-TRAUMATIC GROWTH

Post-traumatic growth is not only a process; it's also an outcome. The outcome of growth, the endgame, may be described in terms of domains. In 1996, a year after the release of their groundbreaking study on post-traumatic growth, Richard Tedeschi and Lawrence Calhoun developed a twenty-one-item inventory to assess growth using five major domains of post-traumatic growth. These domains included: (1) life appreciation and changed priorities, (2) relational intimacy, (3) personal strength, (4) hopefulness about life's possibilities, and (5) growth in spirituality.[13]

Their research concluded that those who experience post-traumatic growth perceive benefits in some or all of these domains. Benefits include such things as a renewed sense of purpose or meaning or a greater sense of self-worth. One can measure the presence and degree of growth by testing for changes in these domains using the twenty-one-item inventory.

The Effects of Post-traumatic Growth on Spirituality

Some studies indicate that traumatized people reported more emotional or spiritual growth than those who were not traumatized. In other words, trauma stimulated growth. Pain, more often than not, is the gateway to spiritual, mental, and emotional gain and positive change. I believe God often uses pain to get our attention and stimulate growth.

Among the many positive changes traumatized people may experience, changes in spirituality are significant. Such changes include spiritual adjustments and new perspectives about the direction of one's life and one's attachment to things.[14] In interviews I conducted for this book, slightly over half the respondents (16/30) reported some form of personal or spiritual growth because of their combat experience. Nine Soldiers specifically stated that they became stronger, more capable of dealing with life's demands, less stressed, and more determined because of their combat experience.[15] In a survey I conducted with 165 Soldiers, 54 percent believed they had become stronger because of their combat experience; 51 percent felt they could grow despite or because of their wartime trauma.[16]

The presence of spirituality in a person contributes to post-traumatic growth. Spiritual people respond more positively to trauma and often deepen their relationships with others because of trauma.[17] They frequently attribute their spiritual growth to a relationship with God, spiritual practices, or the support of a faith community.[18]

In studies I did with veterans of OIF and OEF, some aspect of spirituality or growth was identified as an outcome of their wartime experience. While many stated they believed in God, many were not practicing their spirituality in any formalized setting. Some indicated problems reengaging their faith and reestablishing spiritual practices after returning home. Most felt indebted to God for preserving their lives or acknowledged the presence of a Supreme Being who was with them during combat. Most expressed an appreciation for life, their families, and the protection of God. A few who reported a vibrant faith before, during, and after combat found less difficulty with post-trauma symptoms across all ranges of combat exposure.[19]

ACCESSING SPIRITUAL RESOURCES

Access to spiritual resources mitigates the negative effects of spiritual trauma and contributes to growth.[20] The use of spiritual resources and the possession of religious values or beliefs give the individual a framework for reappraising events in a positive way. This not only opens the gateway for understanding trauma or coping with a traumatic event, but also leads to positive outcomes or growth.

Spirituality produces growth by equipping the sufferer with resources, including forgiveness, mercy, love, and reconciliation. Christian spirituality in particular teaches us about compassion and comfort. We learn about spirituality within the context of the church, where life is affirmed, weaknesses are acknowledged, and faith is encouraged.

EMBRACING THE CHALLENGES

Research on suffering points to the valuable lessons gained through suffering and the evidence of growth.[21] Life is a school of learning, and as people learn to cope, they are propelled forward to growth. Suffering, as part of life, is a means to emotional and spiritual growth, creating an opening in the soul that looks for answers to profound questions. It leads to insights that, prior to the trauma, were obscure and unknown.[22]

Embracing the challenges produced by suffering is the means of discerning one's true self—that is, who one truly is before God. Confronting one's true self is not intended to be easy or painless. It is fraught with uncertainty and tenuousness, but it opens a door to discoveries, new realizations about one's self, and one's capacity to live fully and authentically.[23]

MEANING AND UNDERSTANDING

Post-traumatic spiritual growth acknowledges the presence of meaning and existential changes in suffering.[24] One's search for meaning or significance in suffering is a critical aspect of growth. When victims assign meaning to their trauma, they find healing, and healing suggests growth. It is likely that a change of perspective and an increase in understanding about a traumatic event are predictors of growth. This is implied from a study on post-traumatic growth among victims of the September 11, 2001, attacks. The findings of the study suggest the victims of the attack who acquired a positive view were likely to experience post-traumatic growth.[25]

Spirituality provides the values and moral framework by which one may understand suffering. Belief in God enables a person to know God's presence and God's love. It gives a person a perspective that provides for lasting hope, a perspective on realities that remain certain but are not yet. Spirituality reduces anxiety about death and provides comfort in our suffering. It teaches about loss and limitations. Accepting and nurturing spirituality frees one from the burden of needing to understand everything.[26]

Post-traumatic Growth and Studies on Veterans

It is unclear to what extent combat exposure contributes to post-traumatic growth. However, in some research with combat veterans, there is an indication of growth following intense combat exposure.[27] Several studies reported military service contributes to growth and maturity among servicemembers.[28] Studies conducted on a sample of World War II and Korean veterans who were engaged in heavy combat found that these veterans matured as a result of their wartime experience, exhibiting an increase in coping skills, personal discipline, and perspective on life.[29]

Some findings revealed a coexistence of negative outcomes and positive factors among the sampled population. There was growth, but there was also the presence of negative stress effects, perhaps lingering guilt and grief. Confronted with mortality and the uncertainties of war, some veterans have reported renewed interest in life goals and priorities.[30] J. Glenn Gray and E. B. Sledge both reported renewed interest in goals and priorities due to their combat experience. Gray, already highly educated when he entered the service in World War II, went on to teach philosophy at Colorado College and authored several books. Sledge attended what is now Auburn University and later earned his doctorate in biology from the University of Florida. He likewise became a professor and author.

Recent studies of Vietnam and Gulf War I (1990–1991) veterans have been ambiguous. One study examined several levels of post-traumatic growth reported by Gulf War I veterans using the five domains of growth developed by Richard Tedeschi and Lawrence Calhoun.[31] The results indicated that perceived combat threat was the strongest predictor of an appreciation of life. The availability and quality of social support following deployment contributed to improved relationships, personal strengths, and post-traumatic growth as a whole.

Other studies have found positive connections between social support and post-traumatic growth.[32] In my own research with veterans from OIF and OEF, I found similar evidence of support for post-traumatic growth.[33] Post-traumatic growth is more likely among those without direct or heavy combat exposure. More intense exposure frequently produced negative consequences, and it was unclear from some studies whether those suffering from PTSD would ultimately experience growth as an outcome of combat exposure.[34]

Some studies showed that psychological benefits, particularly solidarity with others, were stronger among those with intermediate combat exposure, as compared to higher or lower levels.[35] Yet other findings revealed post-traumatic growth among veterans who had been exposed to heavy combat.[36]

So the research shows mixed results. The presence of PTSD does not inhibit growth in all veterans; however, when veterans are able to reappraise their trauma in constructive ways and derive meaning from it, then there is a better likelihood of post-trauma growth.

Post-traumatic Growth and Grief

In research on post-traumatic growth and grief, Richard Tedeschi and Lawrence Calhoun examined the consequences of grief and loss and found that many people who were able to accept their losses also experienced various kinds of growth. Becoming reconciled to loss opened the door to considering new possibilities, opportunities to pursue new relationships, and a renewed appreciation for life and its meaning.[37] Individuals reporting positive spiritual changes indicated a new sense of purpose in life and a satisfactory connection to the Transcendent.

NOTES

1. G. Botelho, "What Pride to be Chilean: Rescue Effort Galvanizes Chilean Citizens," *CNN Latin America*, October 14, 2010, accessed December 20, 2015 http://www.cnn.com/2010/WORLD/americas/10/13/chile.miners. national.pride/. See also M. Castillo, "Rescued Miner Says He Saw God, Devil During Captivity," *CNN Latin America*, October 13, 2010, accessed April 2, 2012, http://www.cnn.com/2010/WORLD/americas/10/13/chile. miners.voices/index; E. C. McLaughlin "Hope, Faith Sustain Miners in Chile After Months Below," *CNN World*, October 12, 2010, accessed April 2, 2012, http://edition.cnn.com/2010/WORLD/americas/10/12/chile.miner.rescue. walkup/.

2. CNN Wire Staff, "Everyone Out of the Mine in Chile," *CNN Latin America*, October 14, 2010, accessed April 3, 2012, http://archive.is/TXmA.

3. Richard G. Tedeschi and Lawrence G. Calhoun, *Trauma and Transformation: Growing in the Aftermath of Suffering*, (Thousand Oaks, CA: Sage Publications, 1995); R. G. Tedeschi and L. G. Calhoun, "The Posttraumatic Growth Inventory: Measuring the Positive Legacy of Trauma," *Journal of Traumatic Stress* 9 (1996): 455–471; A. Fontana and R. Rosenheck, "Psychological Benefits and Liabilities of Traumatic Exposure in the War Zone," *Journal of Traumatic Stress* 11, no. 3 (1998): 485–503; Shira Maguen, Dawne Vogt, Lynda King, Daniel King, and Brett Litz, "Posttraumatic Growth Among Gulf War I Veterans: The Predictive Role of Deployment-related Experiences and Background Characteristics," *Journal of Loss and Trauma* 11, (2006): 373–388; Park and Ai, "Meaning Making and Growth."

4. Joseph and Linley, "Psychological Assessment."

5. For example, see Tedeschi and Calhoun, *Trauma and Transformation*; Tedeschi and Calhoun, "The Posttraumatic Growth Inventory"; C. Aldwin and M. Levenson, "Posttraumatic Growth: A Developmental Perspective," *Psychological Inquiry* 15 (2004); Morland et al., "Resilience."

6. A. Mahoney et al., "Broken Vows."

7. Maguen et al., "Posttraumatic Growth."

8. See http://thinkexist.com/quotes/with/keyword/crisis/.

9. Maguen et al., "Posttraumatic Growth."

10. Joseph and Linley, "Psychological Assessment." See also Tedeschi and Calhoun, *Trauma and Transformation*; Tedeschi and Calhoun, "The Posttraumatic Growth Inventory."

11. Tedeschi and Calhoun, "The Posttraumatic Growth Inventory."

12. Pargament et al., "The Sacred."

13. Aldwin and Levenson, "Posttraumatic Growth," 19; Tedeschi and Calhoun, *Trauma and Transformation*; Tedeschi and Calhoun, "The Posttraumatic Growth Inventory."

14. Schiraldi, *The Post-traumatic Stress*.

15. Bonura, "A Biblical Approach."

16. Ibid.

17. Mahoney et al., "Broken Vows."
18. Ibid.
19. Bonura, "A Biblical Approach."
20. Mahoney et al., "Broken Vows"; A. Shaw, S. Joseph, and P. A. Linley, "Religion, Spirituality, and Posttraumatic Growth: A Systematic Review," *Mental Health, Religion & Culture* 8, no. 1 (2005): 3; Plante, "What Do the Spiritual." See also Schiraldi, *The Post-Traumatic Stress.*
21. Paulson, "The Hard Issues."
22. Rankow, "The Transformation of Suffering."
23. Paulson, "The Hard Issues."
24. Morland et al., "Resilience."
25. Ibid.
26. Schiraldi, *The Post-Traumatic Stress.*
27. See for example Maguen et al., "Posttraumatic Growth"; Elder and Clipp, "Combat Experience."
28. As cited in Maguen et al., "Posttraumatic Growth."
29. Elder and Clipp, "Combat Experience."
30. Ibid.
31. Maguen et al., "Posttraumatic Growth."
32. As cited in Maguen et al., "Posttraumatic Growth."
33. D. Bonura, "A Biblical Approach."
34. As cited in Maguen et al., "Posttraumatic Growth."
35. Fontana and Rosenheck, "Psychological Benefits."
36. Elder and Clipp, "Combat Experience."
37. Richard G. Tedeschi and Lawrence G. Calhoun, "Beyond the Concept of Recovery: Growth and the Experience of Loss," *Death Studies* 32 (2008).

Copyright page continued